BOX SCORE CHALLENGE

Logic Puzzles for Baseball Fans

By Joe Eilerman

Volume 2

Relive moments from some of baseball's greatest teams
and players as you attempt to reconstruct a game from
the past using the clues hidden in the box score.

Table of Contents

Introduction

At an early age, I developed a morning ritual shared by countless baseball fans; breakfast came with a quick perusal of the sports page, specifically the box scores. Before the pop-tart sprang from the toaster, I knew whether Aaron had homered the night before, how many hits Rose had collected, and the number of batters Gibson had fanned. With hardly enough patience to fill a thimble, I had no desire to read the lengthy accounts of the game provided by the beat writers. Those few square inches of newsprint dedicated to the box scores delivered all the insight I needed.

Years later, I developed an even greater appreciation of these game summaries and realized the veracity of author Stanley Cohen when he wrote, "The box score is the catechism of baseball, ready to surrender its truth to the knowing eye." With baseball's mano-a-mano structure, pitcher versus batter, the box score allows one to reconstruct the game's events. One player's success is another's failure. A home run by Mays earns him a hit, a run scored, and an RBI, while Seaver is charged with an earned run. A strike-out a few innings later, gets Mays nothing more than a failed at-bat, while Seaver is awarded with another third of an inning pitched. Meshing each of the hitters' batting lines against those of the hurlers' pitching lines, it's possible to discern the outcome of each plate appearance during the entire contest.

While historians may dispute its origins, the National Baseball Hall of Fame enshrined Henry Chadwick as the "inventor" of the box score. This may be equal in myth to the idea of Abner Doubleday as the creator of baseball. Chadwick's version of a condensed game summary came fourteen years after the baseball box score first appeared in the New York Herald, on October 22, 1845. The style and substance suggested a strong link to baseball's British-born cousin, cricket, as only runs scored and outs made were recorded for each batter. It provided no insight into the pitchers' performance other than how they fared at the plate.

Chadwick introduced his concept of the box score to readers of the New York Clipper in 1859, chronicling a game between the Stars and Excelsiors of Brooklyn. He captured the uniqueness of America's game by including the number of hits and runs scored for each batter along with the defensive metrics of put-outs, assists, and errors. He also devoted a single line to convey the teams' collective pitching effectiveness by introducing the term "earned runs."

From its origin of a simple two-stat summary of players' performance, the box score morphed into today's version through a series of changes devised by sports writers to reflect the evolution of the game and to indulge fans' shifting interest. The fascination with the home run and extra bases led to additional notes posted below the batting lines to disclose those hits that went for more than a single. The growing reliance upon relief pitchers brought about individual pitching lines as opposed to the simple summary of a team's collective pitching results. As fans clamored primarily for the offensive numbers of the position players and as a matter of conserving space in the newsprint, individual defensive stats were eventually dismissed from the box score. And as a nod to today's stat cast era, hitters' updated season OPS is now included in most versions.

Though its style and shape may have changed through the years, the fans' addiction to the box score remains constant. It's easy to understand the value of the box score in the early days as baseball grew into America's game. Day games prevented most working-class fans from visiting the ballpark. Long before radio, television, or the Internet, newspapers presented the only means to quelch fans' craving for game-day results. Unable to afford enough time to devour lengthy accounts of the numerous contests, readers needed a quick and concise recap. The box score was practically the sole source to meet that need.

Today, fans can catch most games live on TV. Streaming highlights are available at their fingertips or through twenty-four-hour sports networks. And yet, the box score endures. Maybe that is by some romantic attachment amongst the baseball purists that reminds us of our youth and how we started each day of our summer.

The purpose of this book is to deepen your appreciation of the box score and challenge you to unlock its secrets. Rather than just seeing Aaron clubbed a home run, discover who else may have scored on his round-tripper. Instead of just counting Rose's hits, determine in which innings those occurred and if he ultimately came around to score. And aside from simply taking note of Gibson's strikeouts, determine how many batters in a row he may have retired.

How to Play

Using the information and clues provided from historic box scores, your challenge is to record the timing and results of each hitter at-bat. Since the box score does not reveal all details of the game, you will use a simplified scoring approach as described below.

For each hitter's plate appearance, record in the appropriate inning the results of the at-bat, using all the applicable events.

X - Batter failed to reach base. Whether the result of a groundout, pop-out, strikeout, etc., simply record it as an out. This would also be used to record a hitter who reached base but was subsequently retired while trying to stretch a hit into an extra base or caught stealing. For batters hitting into a double play, indicate as "XX."

H - Signifies a hit, whether a single, double, triple, or home run.

W - Hitter reached on a Base-on-Balls (BB), commonly referred to as a walk. This includes those walked intentionally by the pitcher (IBB).

HBP - Batter was hit by a pitch.

E - Hitter reached base on an error.

FC - Hitter reached on a fielder's choice.

SF - Batter was retired on a fly ball but a runner was able to score on the play.

SH - Batter purposely grounds out, usually by bunting, to advance a runner.

R - Batter scored a run.

I - The batter drove in a run during the at-bat. If more than one run is driven in during the at-bat, precede the I with the number of RBIs.

When completed, the scoring should match the results of both the hitters and pitchers posted in the box score as shown in the example below. Note Ruth's batting results per inning align with the box score summary of five at-bats, one run scored, two hits, and four RBIs. Likewise, the scoring of the highlighted 5th and 6th innings pitched by Lefty Grove, match with his results of two full innings or six outs recorded, three hits allowed, five earned runs, four walks, and 13 batters faced. Note also, how in the 6th inning, the runs scored per the individual hitter's results match the total of four runs scored per the line score.

Batting	1	2	3	4	5	6	7	8	9	AB	R	H	RBI
Earle Combs CF	X		H	X		W,R	X			4	1	1	0
Mark Koenig SS	X		X		W,X	X		X		4	0	0	0
Babe Ruth RF	H		X		X	H,R,4I		E		5	1	2	4
Lou Gehrig 1B	X			H,R,I	FC,R	W		X		4	2	1	1
Bob Meusel LF		X		X	H,I	X		X		5	0	1	1
Tony Lazzeri 2B		H		E	X		H,R			4	1	2	0
Joe Dugan 3B		H		W		H,R	H,X			3	1	3	0
Johnny Grabowski C		XX		X		W,R	FC,I			3	1	0	1
Herb Pennock P			X	W						1	0	0	0
Wilcy Moore P						SH,X	X			1	0	0	0
Runs	0	0	0	1	1	4	1	0	x				
Left on Base	1	1	1	3	1	1	1	1	x				

2B: Bob Meusel (off Lefty Grove); Joe Dugan (off Ike Powers)

HR: Lou Gehrig (off Jack Quinn); Babe Ruth (off Lefty Grove)

SH: Wilcy Moore (off Lefty Grove)

HIDP: Johnny Grabowski

2-Out RBI: Babe Ruth 4; Bob Meusel

Team LOB: 10

Reached on an Error: Tony Lazzeri; Babe Ruth

Reached on a FC: Lou Gehrig

FC Produced an RBI: Johnny Grabowski

Hint : The Yankees left runners on base each inning

Pitching	IP	H	R	ER	BB	BF
Rube Walberg	3	4	0	0	0	12
Jack Quinn	0.1	1	1	1	1	4
Sam Gray	0.2	0	0	0	1	3
Lefty Grove	2	3	5	5	4	13
Ike Powers	2	2	1	1	0	9

Understanding the Box Score

<u>Hitter's Batting Line</u>

AB- At-Bats. Note that AB differs from Plate Appearances as the hitter is not charged with an at-bat in instances of a walk, hit-by-pitch, sacrifice-hit or sacrifice fly.

R – Runs scored by the batter.

H – Hits recorded by the batter.

RBI – Runs-Batted-In by the batter. Note that the batter is not credited with an RBI in the event a run scores during a double play into which the batter hit.

<u>Pitcher's Line</u>

IP – Innings Pitched. The pitcher is credited with a full inning for every three outs he records. Hence, if a pitcher recorded six outs spread out over three innings, he is credited with 2.0 innings pitched. If the total number of outs recorded is not divisible by three, the remainder of one or two is represented after the decimal point. So, for instance, if the pitcher retired 17 batters, he is credited with 5.2 innings pitched.

H – Hits allowed by the pitcher.

R – Runs scored by batters that the pitcher faced. So, for instance, if Pitcher A gave up a base-hit to a batter who then scored after Pitcher B came in as relief during the inning, the run is still charged to Pitcher A.

ER – Earned Runs allowed by the pitcher. This statistic excludes those runs scored because of an error. To determine whether a run was earned or unearned, one must reconstruct the inning as though no errors were committed. Any runs which would not have scored had no errors been committed, are considered unearned. For example, if a hitter reaches base because of an error with two outs and the next batter homers, both runs are unearned as the inning would have ended before the home run had it not been for the error. If, however, there had been only one out when the hitter reached on the error, one run is earned while the other is unearned. The unearned run is because the first runner should not have been on base, save for the error. The second run is earned as, even if the prior batter had been retired, the inning still would have extended to the home run hitter.

BB – Base on Balls issued by the pitcher. Commonly referred to as walks, this statistic also includes intentional base on balls (IBB).

BF – Batters Faced by the pitcher.

<u>Notes to the Box Score</u>

Additional information regarding events of the game may be disclosed in the notes to the box score. While the terms defined below are standard fare in a published box score, other self-explanatory notes or hints have been added to assist in solving the puzzles. The exclusion of any such event defined below from the puzzle box scores does not necessarily mean it did not occur. If, for instance, a stolen base (SB) or intentional walk (IBB) has no bearing on the ability to solve the puzzle, it will not be disclosed in the notes.

Extra base hits are disclosed in the notes; double (2B), triple (3B), and home run (HR).

SF – Sacrifice Fly

*SF – During certain periods, the sacrifice fly was not a recognized statistic. While batters were credited with an RBI, they were also charged with an at-bat. For those games played during periods in which the SF was not recognized, the official box score has been modified so as not to charge the hitter with an at-bat.

SH – Sacrifice Hit

2-Out RBI – Batter drove in run(s) while there were two outs already recorded in the inning.

Team LOB – The number of runners Left-On-Base for the team throughout the game.

IBB- Intentional Base on Balls.

HIDP – Hit Into Double Play.

SB – Stolen Base

HBP – Hit By Pitch

Helpful Hints

Though a batter may reach base on an error or fielder's-choice, he is not credited with a hit but is charged an at-bat.

If a runner reaches base, you may assume that he either scored or was left on base at the end of the inning. Any hitters retired after reaching base safely, such as those caught stealing or attempting to take an extra base will be disclosed in the notes to the box score. Those reaching on a fielder's-choice or hitting into a double-play will also be disclosed so that you are able to discern which runners were erased.

It is not necessary to solve the puzzle in chronological order. In fact, it is usually better to start in the later innings when a relief pitcher enters and throws to only a few batters. Also, innings in which runs are scored, typically make it easier to discern how events unfolded.

Use the Batters Faced (BF) number in the pitching lines to determine which pitchers faced which batters.

If working the inning backward, three outs do not necessarily mean the end of the inning. Batters preceding the first out may have reached base.

Take note of the 2-out RBIs disclosed in the notes to the box score. Having some insight into the number of outs recorded at the time of runs scored can prove invaluable in reconstructing the inning.

Record the runners left on base for each inning and compare your count to the Team LOB figure provided in the notes to the box score as an additional means to confirm the accuracy of your completed scorecard.

Before attempting to complete your first puzzle, consider visiting https://youtu.be/ecX66YduJQ4 for an introductory video; walk through the solutions provided for some of the other puzzles, to develop an understanding of the logic used in completing the scorecards or begin with some of the easier puzzles. Levels of difficulty are indicated in the Table of Contents as such:

✮ Easy

✮✮ Moderate

✮✮✮ Difficult

Puzzles

1. Murderer's Row – 1927 New York Yankees

Few teams have simultaneously dominated the diamond on both offense and defense such as the 1927 New York Yankees. With the likes of Babe Ruth and Lou Gehrig in the middle of the batting order and Herb Pennock and Waite Hoyt topping the rotation, the Yankees scored 371 more runs than they allowed, a mark that only the 1939 Yankees have surpassed during baseball's modern era.

History has shined a much brighter light on the offense as perhaps no other line-up struck more fear into the hearts of opposing pitchers. Powered by a group of six atop the order dubbed Murderers' Row, the Yankees pushed a major league, leading 976 runners across the plate, for an astounding average of 6.3 runs per game. They also led all of baseball in triples, home runs, RBIs, and walks. As a team, they slashed .307/.384/.488 with an OPS of .872, which surpassed the second-best team by nearly 100 points.

Legends Gehrig and Ruth cemented the heart of the batting order. The two combined for 107 home runs during the season, which nearly doubled the 56 smacked by the Philadelphia Athletics who owned the second-highest number of team home runs in the American League. Gehrig amassed 218 hits, knocked in a league-leading 173 runs, clubbed 47 home runs, and posted a staggering OPS of 1.240 while winning the AL MVP Award. Ruth set the high-water mark for home runs in a single season with 60 while driving in 165 runs and besting Gehrig with an OPS of 1.258. At the top of the order, Earle Combs and Mark Koenig set the table before the two stalwarts. Combs batted .356 while leading the league with 231 hits and combined with Koenig to score 236 runs. Bob Meusel and Tony Lazzeri rounded out the core group. Despite batting behind Ruth and Gehrig, they managed to clean up the few crumbs left on base, driving in an excess of 100 runs apiece.

The Yankees suffered only one shut-out during the year, a late-season loss at the hands of Lefty Grove and the Philadelphia Athletics. They more than made up for this deprivation, however, with a fireworks display during a 4th of July doubleheader against the visiting Washington Senators, in front of 72,641 spectators. After banging out 18 hits in winning the first game by a score of 12-1, they followed with a barrage of 19 hits and 11 walks to take the nightcap, 21-1.

Though the offense grabbed the headlines, the pitching also proved stellar with a major league-best 3.20 ERA. Hoyt tied for the American League lead in winning 22 games with fellow starters Pennock, contributing 19, and Urban Shocker, 18. While mostly coming out of the bullpen, rookie Wilcy Moore also contributed 19 wins and led the majors in saves with 13. All four finished in the top ten amongst AL hurlers in both wins and ERA, with Moore's 2.28 winning the ERA title.

With the major's most explosive offense and stingiest defense, the Yankees easily captured the AL pennant with a record of 110 - 44. They went wire-to-wire, remaining atop the league for the entire season, and bested the second-place Philadelphia Athletics by 19 games. Their dominance continued in the postseason, blanking the Pittsburgh Pirates four games to none for the franchise's second World Series Championship.

Cooperstown helped to immortalize this team with seven inductees: Ruth, Gehrig, Combs, Lazzeri, Pennock, Hoyt, and manager, Miller Huggins.

Here's a game from August 25 of that year showcasing the potency of the Yankee line-up as they gathered 13 hits and 7 walks against the Detroit Tigers. Despite stranding 11 runners on base, the Yankees plated eight runs to knock off the Tigers and improve their record to 84-37. Herb Pennock went the full nine innings for the Yankees, allowing seven hits and issuing two walks. He gave up only two runs in securing his 13th win of the season. The victory was the second amid an 8-game-win streak that ultimately pushed the Yankee's lead to 18 games in the AL standings by September 2.

New York Yankees at Detroit Tigers
   August 25, 1927

Batting	1	2	3	4	5	6	7	8	9	AB	R	H	RBI
Earle Combs CF										6	1	2	0
Mark Koenig SS										5	2	2	0
Babe Ruth LF										2	1	0	0
Lou Gehrig 1B										4	2	2	4
Bob Meusel RF										4	1	1	1
Tony Lazzeri 2B										4	0	2	1
Joe Dugan 3B										5	0	3	1
Benny Bengough C										2	0	0	0
Cedric Durst PH										1	0	0	0
Pat Collins C										1	0	0	0
Herb Pennock P										4	1	1	1
Runs	0	1	0	0	4	2	0	0	1				
Left on Base													

2B: Joe Dugan (off Earl Whitehill); Herb Pennock (off Don Hankins); Tony Lazzeri (off Rip Collins)
HR: Lou Gehrig (off Earl Whitehill)
SF: Tony Lazzeri (off George Smith)
HIDP: Cedric Durst
2-Out RBI: None
Team LOB: 11
FC Produced an RBI: Herb Pennock
Cedric Durst pinchhit for Benny Bengough in the 5th inning.
Hint: The Yankees left two runners on base in the second.
Hint: Hankins' two walks came in separate innings

Pitching	IP	H	R	ER	BB	BF
Earl Whitehill	4	7	5	5	3	22
George Smith	1	1	0	0	1	4
Don Hankins	2	3	2	2	2	11
Rip Collins	2	2	1	1	1	9

Earl Whitehill faced 4 batters in the 5th inning.

SOLUTION   Murderer's Row – 1927 New York Yankees

Batting	1	2	3	4	5	6	7	8	9	AB	R	H	RBI
Earle Combs CF	X		H		H,R	X	X		X	6	1	2	0
Mark Koenig SS	X		X		H,R	H,R		X		5	2	2	0
Babe Ruth LF	X		W		W,R	W		X		2	1	0	0
Lou Gehrig 1B		H,R,I	X		W,R,I	H,2I		X		4	2	2	4
Bob Meusel RF		X	X		W,I	X			H,R	4	1	1	1
Tony Lazzeri 2B		H		X	SF,I,X	X			H	4	0	2	1
Joe Dugan 3B		H		H	H,I		X		X	5	0	3	1
Benny Bengough C		X		X						2	0	0	0
Cedric Durst PH					XX					1	0	0	0
Pat Collins C							X		W,X	1	0	0	0
Herb Pennock P		X		X		H,R	W		FC,I	4	1	1	1
Runs	0	1	0	0	4	2	0	0	1				
Left on Base	0	2	2	1	2	2	0	0	2				

The Yankees sent forty-six batters to the plate during the game, which means they went through the order five full times, with Combs getting an extra turn. Those charged with fewer at-bats compared with plate appearances, included Lazzeri with an SF and walks to Ruth (3), Gehrig, Meusel, Pennock and someone in the eighth spot of the line-up.

<u>5th Inning</u>

According to the box score, Whitehill pitched to four batters in the 5th. As his official line credited him for only 4 innings pitched, all four batters he faced in the 5th reached base. He pitched to a total of 22 batters, so the last four would have been 19 through 22: Combs, Koenig, Ruth, and Gehrig. Combs and Koenig had no walks during the game, so both had to reach on a hit. Ruth had no hits, so he had to reach on one of his three walks. We will come back to Gehrig.

Smith came in to face the next four batters; Meusel through Durst, who pinch hit for Bengough here in the 5th, and gave up one hit and one walk. Per the notes, Durst hit into a DP in his only at-bat of the game, so of the remaining three batters, one received a walk, one reached on a hit, and the other was retired. Of the three, Meusel was the only one who had a walk during the game, so he received the free pass.

Lazzeri, as disclosed in the notes, had a sacrifice fly off Smith, so he accounted for the out but picked up an RBI.

That then leaves Dugan to have collected the hit.

As all four runs this inning were charged to Whitehall, they had to come from the four batters he faced: Combs, Koenig, Ruth, and Gehrig.

6th Inning

The Yankees scored two more runs this inning. The unaccounted runs scored at this point belong to Pennock, Koenig, and Meusel. Gehrig also had another run to account for, but that came as a result of his home run off Whitehill.

According to the hint, Hankins's walks came in separate innings, so there had to be at least four batters in the 7th: one walk and three outs. Combs was the 37th and final batter faced by Hankins. Thus, at the very least, Dugan would have led off the 7th, leaving Lazzeri to account for the final out of the 6th, and thus no scenario for Meusel to score in the 6th as Lazzeri's RBI is already recorded. Therefore, Pennock and Koenig had to score the two runs this inning.

So Pennock had to reach base with either a hit or a walk.

Combs did not score this inning, so he had to be out prior to Koenig circling the bases.

Koenig received no walks during the game, so he had to reach on one of his two hits before coming around to score.

Note there were no 2-out RBIs during the game. As one out is already in the books and neither Pennock nor Koenig had yet scored when Ruth came to the plate, the Babe had to reach safely so that someone behind him could drive home the runs with less than two outs. As he had no hits, he must have reached on a walk.

Going back to the hint that Hankins' two walks came during separate innings, with Ruth having walked, Pennock had to reach on his double noted in the box score.

As previously noted, four spots in the order must be saved for the 7th inning, meaning of the next three batters, Gehrig, Meusel, and Lazzeri, two account for the remaining two outs to be recorded while the other drives home the two runs.

Noting again that there were no 2-out RBIs, Gehrig had to reach safely on a hit while collecting the two RBIs, leaving Meusel and Lazzeri to account for the final two outs.

<u>Back to the 5th Inning</u>

With one of Gehrig's hits now recorded in the 6th and knowing the other came via the home run off Whitehill disclosed in the notes, Gehrig must have reached on a walk during the 5th. With the bases loaded in front of him, he also picked up an RBI.

Meusel then picked up an RBI on his bases-loaded walk as well, and Dugan drove in the final run of the inning on his hit.

<u>9th Inning</u>

The only unaccounted run scored, other than Gehrig's home run off Whitehill, now belongs to Meusel, so he had to reach base this inning. As his walk is already recorded, he collected his lone hit this inning.

Per the notes, Lazzeri doubled off Collins. As Collins only pitched to nine hitters over his two innings, Lazzeri only faces him once, so the double had to occur this inning.

Pennock has the only unaccounted-for RBI other than Gehrig's which came via the aforementioned home run. So Pennock drove home Meusel this inning with the FC disclosed in the notes.

Combs was the 46th and final batter of the game for the Yankees, so he was out.

To produce the RBI with an FC, there had to be less than two outs when Pennock came to the plate, meaning between Dugan and Pat Collins, one reached base safely and the other accounted for the second out of the inning. As both hits charged to Rip Collins are accounted for, the runner had to reach on the lone walk issued by Rip Collins. As Pat Collins is the only one of the two who received a free pass, he reached base while Dugan was retired.

Whether it was Lazzeri or Collins who was forced out on Pennock's FC is inconsequential to the scoring, but per official records, it was Collins who was retired.

<u>8th Inning</u>

Collins pitched to a total of nine batters in the 8th and 9th. As six of those are already accounted for in the 9th, the remaining three accounted for the three outs in the 8th: Koenig, Ruth, and Gehrig.

<u>7th Inning</u>

Of the four batters this inning, one had to reach on the second walk issued by Hankins. As Pennock is the only one of the four with an unaccounted-for walk, he received the base-on-balls while the other three accounted for the outs.

1st Inning

Gehrig's home run had to have come in the 2nd as that is the only remaining inning with unaccounted-for runs. Thus, all three batters in the first were set down in order.

2nd Inning

As noted above, Gehrig led off the inning with a home run.

Meusel was out, as his walk and hit are already recorded.

Per the hint, two runners were left on base this inning, meaning that of the next four batters, two reached base, and two were out. Of those four, Bengough and Pennock have no remaining hits or walks to record, so they were both retired. Neither Lazzeri nor Dugan drew a walk during the game, so both reached on hits.

3rd and 4th Innings

Combs reached on a base hit and Ruth walked during the 3rd while Koenig, Gehrig, and Meusel accounted for the outs to complete their lines.

During the 4th, Dugan collected the second of his three hits with Lazzeri, Bengough, and Pennock each retired to complete their lines.

2. The Big Red Machine – 1975 and 1976 Cincinnati Reds

The Cincinnati Reds of the 1970s earned the title of "The Big Red Machine" based on a relentless offense and the ability to churn out wins. Throughout the decade, they averaged 95 wins a season and led all of baseball with a winning percentage of .592. They collected six National League Western Division titles, four pennants, and two World Series championships.

The apex of their dominance came in 1975 and 1976 with the assemblage of the "Great Eight": Pete Rose, Joe Morgan, Johnny Bench, Tony Perez, Dave Concepcion, George Foster, Cesar Geronimo, and Ken Griffey, Sr. With this lethal line-up intact, the Reds led all of baseball in runs scored during both campaigns, averaging more than five tallies per game. During the '76 regular season, the Reds topped the majors in nearly all offensive categories including hits, doubles, triples, home runs, RBIs, walks, total bases, batting average, and on-base and slugging percentages. But they could also flash the leather, evidenced by the collective 25 Gold Gloves earned throughout their careers, eight of those during the '75 and '76 seasons.

With such an assortment of 2-way talent, Cincinnati posted 108 wins in 1975 and clinched the NL Western Division by 20 games. After sweeping the Pirates in the NL Championship Series, they knocked off the Boston Red Sox in seven games to claim the franchise's first World Series title since 1940. The following year, they became the first NL team to win back-to-back Championships since the '21 and '22 New York Giants after winning 102 games in the regular season and again sweeping the NLCS.

With the star-studded cast at his disposal, manager, Sparky Anderson acquired a misinformed reputation of simply rubber-stamping his line-up from day to day. But the Great Eight started together in only 80 regular season games. That the Reds won 64 of those games enriches the argument of this group as the most successful line-up in MLB history and perhaps questions why Anderson didn't, in fact, use a Xerox to fill in his scorecard.

Rose provided the spark at the top of the line-up, collecting over 200 hits and leading the majors in runs scored during each of the two championship years. Griffey supplemented Rose as a fellow table setter, reaching base at nearly a .400 clip and scoring 206 runs during the two seasons. Opposing pitchers then faced a gauntlet that virtually ensured a run scored if either of the two prior batters reached base. Morgan drove in 205 runs during the two-year window while leading all of baseball with an OPS of .974 in 1975 and again in 1976 with a mark of 1.020. He took home MVP honors both years along with his two Gold Gloves. Johnny Bench, who netted MVP Awards in '70 and '72, continued his steady production with another 184 RBIs over the '75 and '76 seasons, while Perez picked up an even 200 and Foster knocked in 199.

While Pete Rose's off-field antics have kept him away from Cooperstown, the Big Red Machine's legacy endures with the inductions of Morgan, Bench, and Perez into the Hall of Fame.

Here's an early-season game from the 1976 season in which the Reds defeated the visiting Houston Astros by a score of 9-3. Pete Rose accounted for four of the Reds' 13 hits while each of the eight position players, save for Concepcion, had at least one RBI. Pitcher, Pat Darcy, went 5.1 innings for the Reds, giving up all three of Houston's runs on only two hits and two walks. Pat Zachry and Will McEnaney closed out the remainder of the game to keep the Reds undefeated at 3-0.

Houston Astros at **Cincinatti Reds**

April 11, 1976

Batting	1	2	3	4	5	6	7	8	9	AB	R	H	RBI
Pete Rose 3B										6	2	4	1
Ken Griffey RF										3	2	1	1
Joe Morgan 2B										4	1	2	2
Johnny Bench C										4	1	0	1
Tony Perez 1B										5	0	1	2
George Foster LF										3	1	1	1
Dave Concepcion SS										3	0	0	0
Cesar Geronimo CF										5	0	1	1
Pat Darcy P										3	1	2	0
Pat Zachry P										1	1	1	0
Mike Lum PH										1	0	0	0
Runs	2	0	0	4	0	0	1	2	x				
Left on Base													

2B: Joe Morgan (off Joe Niekro); Tony Perez (off Joaquin Andujar); Pete Rose (off Mike Barlow);
Cesar Geronimo (off Mike Barlow)

2-Out RBI: Tony Perez

Team LOB: 13

Reached on an Error: Johnny Bench

Johnny Bench and Tony Perez each picked up an RBI on a groundout, but not in the same inning.

Hint: *The only two battters that received back-to-back walks were Foster and Concepcion*

Pitching	IP	H	R	ER	BB	BF
Joe Niekro	3.1	6	6	6	5	21
Joaquin Andujar	1.2	3	0	0	1	9
Joe Sosa	1	0	0	0	1	4
Mike Barlow	1.1	4	3	2	1	10
Larry Hardy	0.2	0	0	0	0	2

SOLUTION   The Big Red Machine – 1975 and 1976 Cincinnati Reds

Batting	1	2	3	4	5	6	7	8	9	AB	R	H	RBI
Pete Rose 3B	H,R	X		H,R	H		H,I	X		6	2	4	1
Ken Griffey RF	W,R	X		H,R,I	W		X			3	2	1	1
Joe Morgan 2B	H,I		W	H,R,I	X		X			4	1	2	2
Johnny Bench C	X		X	X,I		W		E,R		4	1	0	1
Tony Perez 1B	X,I		X	H,I		X		X		5	0	1	2
George Foster LF	W		W	X		X		H,R,I		3	1	1	1
Dave Concepcion SS	W		X		X	X		W		3	0	0	0
Cesar Geronimo CF	X			X	X		X	H,I		5	0	1	1
Pat Darcy P		X		H,R	H					3	1	2	0
Pat Zachry P							H,R			1	1	1	0
Mike Lum PH								X		1	0	0	0
Runs	2	0	0	4	0	0	1	2	x				
Left on Base	3	0	2	1	3	1	1	2	x				

With the Reds having sent 46 batters to the plate during the game, each position in the order came to the plate five times, save for Rose who had six plate appearances. Those charged with fewer at-bats than plate appearances were Morgan and Bench who each drew a walk and Griffey, Foster, and Concepcion who each received two free passes.

7TH and 8th Innings

Larry Hardy entered during the 8th and threw to the final two batters of the game, Lum and Rose. Both were retired as Hardy gave up no hits or walks during his brief appearance.

Barlow came in to start the 7th and faced the 35th batter, Geronimo. Per the notes, Geronimo doubled off Barlow at some point. That double was Geronimo's only means of producing his RBI, however. Leading off the 7th, a double could not have driven in a run, so Geronimo's extra-base hit and RBI had to come the following inning in his second try against Barlow. His at-bat here in the 7th resulted in an out as he had no other hits or walks for the game.

Zachary followed Geronimo to the plate during the 7th for his only at-bat of the game and per his batting line, he reached on a hit and eventually came around to score.

Rose also doubled off Barlow. As he faced Barlow only once and he was the third batter of the 7th, Rose's two-bagger occurred during the 7th.

With Rose having reached base, the 7th inning will have to extend to at least Morgan to account for the final two outs. That leaves only Bench and Foster as the candidates to have scored the two runs during the 8th.

Barlow did give up an unearned run during his outing, so that must have been the result of Bench reaching on the error disclosed in the notes.

Perez's only hit was a double off Andujar and he had no walks, so he was the first out of the 8th. With little chance of Perez having driven Bench home via a ground out this inning, Foster and Geronimo had to pick up the RBIs.

As a walk would not have driven Bench home, Foster had to reach on his lone hit before coming around to score on Geronimo's double.

Concepcion had to reach base during the 8th to extend the inning to Rose. As Concepcion had no hits, he received the lone walk issued by Barlow.

Both Griffey and Morgan were retired to end the 7th so that Bench could lead off the 8th. That leaves Rose to have knocked in Zachry to collect his lone RBI.

6th Inning

Concepcion was the final batter faced by Sosa, so he was retired to end the inning.

Of the three preceding batters Sosa faced, he walked one. Either Bench or Foster drew that walk, but as Perez received no free passes during the game, he was out.

4th Inning

Andujar came in during the 4th inning with one out already recorded. The second batter he faced was Perez and per the notes, he doubled at some point off Andujar. As this was his only opportunity in facing Andujar, Perez had to pick up the double this inning.

As Andujar was not charged with any runs for the game, all four tallies this inning were owned by Niekro. That means, each of those scoring this inning had to reach base before Andujar came in to face his first batter, Johnny Bench. That leaves Darcy, Rose, Griffey, and Morgan to have crossed the plate this inning.

As neither Darcy nor Rose drew a walk during the game, they had to reach on base-hits this inning before scoring.

Niekro did record one out during the inning and as Geronimo's lone hit is already recorded, he accounted for the first out of the frame.

Perez had two RBIs for the game, but only one came with two outs, thus they had to come in separate innings. One of those RBIs had to come with his lone hit here in the 4th. Per the notes, the other RBI came on a groundout, which obviously could not have come with two outs. Thus, Perez's other RBI had to come during the 1st inning on the ground out, as that is the only remaining frame in which the Reds scored.

To create the 2-out RBI opportunity for Perez this inning, Bench had to account for the second out of the 4th. But with the first inning as Bench's only other possibility to drive home a run on a ground out, and Perez having already done exactly that, the notes tell us that Bench had to collect his RBI here in the 4th.

With Rose's and Foster's RBIs already recorded, the only two candidates for the remaining RBIs are Griffey and Morgan. As Morgan was credited with knocking in two runs during the game, and Perez accounted for one of the two in the 1st, Morgan had to collect at least one RBI this inning, meaning, he reached on a hit before scoring himself.

5th Inning

Andujar gave up two more hits over the seven remaining batters he faced. Foster, Geronimo, Griffey, and Morgan all have their hits recorded already, leaving Darcy and Rose as the only two candidates to have picked up those hits. For the 4th inning to have extended to Darcy, both Foster and Concepcion would have had to have reached base and thus loaded the bases for the Reds. Darcy's hit would then have driven in a run, but as Darcy had no RBIs for the game, his hit had to occur in the 5th.

Rose, following Darcy in the line-up, then collected his hit in the 5th as well.

Morgan was the last batter Andujar faced, so he was out to end the inning.

1st Inning

The only two unrecorded runs scored belong to Rose and Griffey, so each had to reach base this inning. As Rose did not draw any walks during the game, he reached on the first of his four base hits before circling the bases.

Griffey had only one hit and one RBI for the game. With Rose having singled and Griffey having no extra-base hits, Griffey could not have driven Rose home this inning. Thus, Griffey's lone hit and RBI had to occur during the 4th inning, and he drew one of his two walks here in the 1st.

With Griffey accounting for one of the RBIs during the 4th, Morgan had to collect the first of his two RBIs here in the 1st on a base hit.

3rd Inning

Concepcion could not have reached base during the 4th inning as he would have scored ahead of Darcy, but he was credited with no runs scored for the game. If he had led off with an out, both Griffey and Morgan would have been credited with a 2-out RBI. But since neither drove in a run with two outs, Concepcion must have ended the 3rd inning with an out.

Tony Perez also had to come to the plate during the 3rd and since his lone hit is already recorded, he was out as well.

Back to the 1st Inning

Relying on the hint that Foster and Concepcion received back-to-back walks at some point in the game, that had to occur here in the 1st inning. The only other possibility was during the 4th, but Andujar gave up only one walk during his outing, so that frame is ruled out.

With Morgan already on base, the two walks loaded the bases. As the Reds two runs scored are already accounted for, Bench could not have been on base when those two walks were issued otherwise Morgan would have been pushed home. Bench was therefore the first out of the inning.

Geronimo was out to end the inning, as his lone hit was already recorded, and he did not draw any walks.

2ⁿᵈ Inning

With Darcy's two hits already recorded, he was out to lead off the inning.

Likewise, all four of Rose's hits were recorded, so he too was out.

Back to the 3ʳᵈ Inning

Morgan has one more plate appearance to account for his walk. For that to have occurred during the 2ⁿᵈ inning, Griffey would have had to reach base to extend the frame to Morgan. But Griffey's only remaining means of reaching base is via a walk. But as the hint disclosed, back-to-back walks occurred only once during this game, and that came in the 1ˢᵗ inning. Therefore, Morgan had to lead off the 3ʳᵈ with his walk, meaning Griffey ended the 2ⁿᵈ with an out.

Relying on the hint once again, though Bench still has a walk to record, it could not have occurred following Morgan's free pass this inning, so he was out.

Foster had to reach base to extend the inning to Concepcion. As his lone hit was already recorded, he drew the fifth and final walk issued by Niekro.

Back to the 4ᵗʰ and 5ᵗʰ Innings

Griffey had to draw a walk during the 5ᵗʰ to complete his line.

With Andujar's three hits and one walk now accounted for, the remaining batters he faced were all retired: Foster during the 4ᵗʰ and Concepcion and Geronimo in the 5ᵗʰ.

Back to the 6ᵗʰ

With Foster's two walks now recorded, he was out, and Bench had to draw the lone free pass issued by Barlow.

3. Jackie Robinson and the Brooklyn Dodgers

Branch Rickey helped to break major league baseball's color barrier by signing Jackie Robinson to a contract with the Brooklyn Dodgers in 1947, but his willingness to challenge the unwritten ban went further than a single player and allowed him to assemble a dominant National League franchise. After he had turned the St. Louis Cardinals into perennial favorites through the development of a farm system, the Dodgers lured Rickey to the east coast in 1943 with the title of Team President. While enduring the loss of several players to military service during his first few years, Ricky began to lay the foundation of a farewell gift to the city of Brooklyn in the form of the franchise's most successful decade.

In 1946, Pee Wee Reese rejoined the team after serving three years in the Navy and showed little signs of rust, playing in 152 games while reaching base at a .384 clip and earning the second of his ten all-star appearances. The following year, Gil Hodges returned from his two years in the Marines and was joined by rookies, Duke Snider and Jackie Robinson. Hodges, who had taken the field as a 19-year-old for only one game prior to enlisting, and Snider were used sparingly during their initial full seasons, but Robinson's performance must have left several general managers lamenting their decision to steer clear of signing any players out of the Negro Leagues. His slash line of .297/.383/.427, 125 runs scored and a league-leading 29 stolen bases, easily garnered MLB's first-ever Rookie-of-the-year Award and a fifth-place showing in the NL MVP voting. Led by Reese and Robinson, along with 21-game winner, Ralph Blanca, the Dodgers posted 94 wins during the regular season and outdistanced Rickey's former St. Louis team for their first pennant in six years.

After losing the World Series in seven games to the New York Yankees, Rickey again looked to the Negro Leagues and brought in Roy Campanella to start the 1948 season and Don Newcombe a year later. With the nucleus now in place, the Dodgers went on a tear during their remaining years in Brooklyn. In the eight seasons, beginning in 1949, they never finished lower than second place and never posted fewer than 89 wins. At the core of this success dwelt an explosive offense fueled by a lethal combination of speed and power. Campanella, Hodges, and Snider combined to average 94 home runs a year during that stretch, exceeding the century mark on four occasions. Robinson, who reached base at a .418 clip during that period, combined with Reese to lead the Dodgers in swiping 20 bases more on average than the other major league teams. The potency of the line-up led to the Dodgers leading the National League in runs scored every year from 1949 to 1955, including the 1953 season in which they averaged an incredible 6.16 tallies a game.

Don Newcombe led the pitching staff and made his presence known immediately, going 17-8 with five shutouts during that 1949 campaign and securing Rookie of the Year honors. Despite missing the '52 and '53 seasons while away on military leave, he contributed four seasons with at least 19 wins during Brooklyn's dominant run, including the 1956 season in which he threw for 268 innings and led all of baseball with 27 wins, six more than his closest competitor.

Individual accolades naturally followed such team success, with Campanella collecting three MVPs ('51, '53, and '54) and Robinson awarded the honors in '50. Newcombe added to the collection of hardware with both the Cy Young and MVP Awards in 1956. Collectively, the core group made 37 all-star appearances from 1949 to 1956, all of them earning invitations in 1950 and 1951 and Campanella participating in all eight. With the Golden Days Era Committee selecting Hodges for enshrinement to the Hall of Fame in 2022, all but Newcombe are now immortalized within the halls of Cooperstown.

Unfortunately for Brooklyn, their stretch of historical success coincided with the cross-town Yankees long run of dominance. The Dodgers claimed six more National League pennants after Robinson's rookie year ('49,

'52, '53, '55, and '56), but like in 1947, they faced the Yankees during the World Series. The city of Brooklyn hoisted the championship trophy only once, in 1955, before departing for Los Angeles in 1958.

Here's a game from late in the '49 season in which the Dodgers clobbered the visiting Philadelphia Phillies 8-1, to improve their record to 94-55 and remain half a game behind the St. Louis Cardinals. Newcombe went the full nine innings, scattering only four hits and walking three while striking out nine. He allowed only one run en route to picking up his 16th win of the season. Five days later, the Dodgers swept a double header with the Boston Braves to take the lead in the National League and went on to win the pennant with a record of 97-57.

Philadelphia Phillies at **Brooklyn Dodgers**
        September 24, 1949

Batting	1	2	3	4	5	6	7	8	9	AB	R	H	RBI
Pee Wee Reese SS										5	1	1	0
Eddie Miksis 3B										5	1	1	0
Carl Furillo RF										3	2	2	2
Jackie Robinson 2B										4	0	1	0
Gil Hodges 1B										3	2	2	1
Luis Olmo LF										2	1	2	2
Gene Hermanski LF										2	0	0	0
Roy Campanella C										3	1	2	2
Duke Snider CF										4	0	1	1
Don Newcombe P										4	0	0	0
Runs	0	1	4	0	0	1	2	0	x				
Left on Base													

HR: Roy Campanella (off Ken Trinkle); Carl Furillo (off Ken Trinkle)
2-Out RBI: Luis Olmo 2; Roy Campanella; Gil Hodges
Team LOB: 6
Runners retired on the bases: Luis Olmo thrown out at 3rd
Hint: Reese collected his base hit before Furillo got either of his two.

Pitching	IP	H	R	ER	BB	BF
Jocko Thompson	2.2	7	5	5	1	15
Russ Meyer	2.1	1	0	0	0	8
Ken Trinkle	1.1	4	3	3	1	9
Curt Simmons	0.2	0	0	0	1	3
Bob Miller	1	0	0	0	0	3

SOLUTION   Jackie Robinson and the Brooklyn Dodgers

Batting	1	2	3	4	5	6	7	8	9	AB	R	H	RBI
Pee Wee Reese SS	X		H,R	X			X	X		5	1	1	0
Eddie Miksis 3B	X		X	X			H,R	X		5	1	1	0
Carl Furillo RF	W		H,R		X		H,R,2I			3	2	2	2
Jackie Robinson 2B	X		X		X		H			4	0	1	0
Gil Hodges 1B		H,R	H,R,I		X		W			3	2	2	1
Luis Olmo LF		H,X	H,R,2I							2	1	2	2
Gene Hermanski LF						X	X			2	0	0	0
Roy Campanella C		X	H,I			H,R,I	W			3	1	2	2
Duke Snider CF		H,I	X			X	X			4	0	1	1
Don Newcombe P		X		X		X		X		4	0	0	0
Runs	0	1	4	0	0	1	2	0	x				
Left on Base	1	1	1	0	0	0	3	0	x				

With the Dodgers having sent 38 batters to the plate during the game, each position in the order had four plate appearances, with the top two getting an extra turn. Those charged with fewer at-bats than plate appearances, included Furillo, Hodges, and Campanella, each having drawn a walk.

8th Inning

Bob Miller faced batters 36 through 38: Newcombe, Reese, and Miksis to end the game. As he gave up no hits or walks, all three were retired.

7th Inning

Simmons pitched to the final three batters of the 7th inning: Hermanski, Campanella, and Snider, giving up one walk and retiring the other two. As Campanella was the only one of these three to have drawn a walk during the game, he got the free pass and the other two were out.

6th Inning

Trinkle came in to start the inning and faced nine hitters beginning with Hermanski. As Hermanski had no hits or walks for the game, he was out.

Per the notes, Campanella hit a home run against Trinkle. That had to occur this inning, as Trinkle faced Campanella only once.

Snider does have an unrecorded hit, but he also has an unrecorded RBI. As there was not an RBI opportunity for him during this inning, the hit had to come at some other time during the game, so he was out this inning.

16

Newcombe had no hits or walks, so he was retired for the final out of the inning.

7th Inning

Trinkle still has five more batters he must face. Per the notes, Furillo hit a home run off Trinkle, so that had to occur during this inning.

That leaves Hodges as the only one who could account for the one walk Trinkle issued.

Either Reese or Miksis had to reach base this inning so that it could extend all the way to Snider. But as the Dodgers scored only two runs this inning, only one of the two could have been on in front of Furillo's home run. Per the hint, Reese got his lone hit before Furillo got either of his two. Given the Dodgers did not collect any hits beyond the 7th inning, Furillo had to collect his first hit before the home run, meaning Reese did not reach base here in the 7th. That leaves Miksis as the one who reached on a hit and scored this inning on the home run, earning Furillo two RBIs. Reese then led off with an out.

To extend the inning past Hermanski, Robinson had to reach base on his lone hit this inning.

3rd Inning

The unrecorded runs at this point belong to Reese, Furillo, Hodges, and Olmo. As the Dodgers pushed four runs across the plate this inning, each of these four accounted for one apiece.

Neither Reese nor Olmo drew a walk during the game, so both had to reach on base-hits before coming around to score.

Hodges's one walk came during the 7th, so he had to reach on a hit as well.

We will come back to determine how Furillo reached base this inning.

Meyer came in with two outs to finish up the 3rd inning after Thompson allowed the hit to Olmo. Someone behind Olmo had to drive him home as he scored one of the runs during the inning as noted above. Both Campanella and Snider have unrecorded RBIs, but only Campanella had a 2-out RBI, so he drove in Olmo with a hit.

As Meyer allowed only one hit during his appearance, Snider was out to end the inning.

Of the other three remaining RBIs this inning, Hodges had to pick up one and Olmo got the other two. The only other unrecorded RBI at this time belongs to Snider, but as noted above, he was the final out of the inning and thus eliminated from consideration.

As Miksis's lone hit is already recorded, he was retired for the first out of the inning.

Likewise, with Robinson's hit accounted for, he was also retired.

Newcombe could not have led off this inning, as he had no hits or walks and would have been out, not allowing the inning to extend past Robinson. He, therefore, made the final out of the 2nd.

4th and 5th Innings

Again, Meyer allowed no further hits or walks so the remaining six batters he faced were all retired beginning with Newcombe in the 4th and ending with Hodges in the 5th.

1st Inning

Reese and Miksis were both out as their hits were already recorded.

Per the hint, Furillo did not collect either of his two hits until after Reese got his. As Reese did not get his hit until the 3rd inning, Furillo had to reach on his walk here in the 1st before collecting the first of his two hits in the 3rd.

Robinson was the third out of the inning to complete his line.

2nd Inning

The only unrecorded run scored belongs to Hodges who had to reach on the first of his two base hits before coming around to score.

The only unrecorded RBI is owned by Snider, so he had to drive in Hodges with his lone base hit.

Per the notes, Olmo was thrown out at third base at some point in the game. The only other inning in which Olmo reached base was the 3rd, but he scored during that frame so, obviously, was not retired on the bases. Thus, he had to reach on the first of his two hits here in the 2nd before being thrown out at third.

Campanella was out to complete his line.

Newcombe as noted earlier, was the final out of the inning.

4. 2001 Seattle Mariners

Despite having reached the AL Championship Series in 2000, the future appeared bleak for the Seattle Mariners. During the off-season, they lost Alex Rodriguez to free agency, adding to the angst suffered with the departure of fellow superstars, Ken Griffey Jr. after the 1999 season and Randy Johnson during the 1998 campaign. Remarkably, a roster of castaways and unproven talents interspersed with the few remaining veterans, did not only exceed expectations but also claimed a piece of history in tying the 1906 Chicago Cubs in posting 116 regular season wins.

Other stars emerged to carry the team, and none shined brighter than Ichiro Suzuki. The former Japanese league star wasted no time in introducing himself to the American game, leading the majors with 242 hits and a .350 batting average while earning Rookie of the Year honors, as well as MVP. Bret Boone, who began his career with Seattle before moving on to three other clubs, averaged 14 home runs and 60 RBIs a year while batting .255, before rejoining the Mariners in 2001. He suddenly became an offensive force, setting career highs in hits (206), home runs (37), RBIs (141), batting average (.331), on-base (.372), and slugging (.578). John Olerud brought his career batting average of .301 to Seattle in 2000 and continued hitting at that clip in 2001, along with 21 home runs and 95 RBIs. Mike Cameron, who came over from Cincinnati in the trade for Ken Griffey Jr, contributed 25 home runs and 110 RBIs and earned a Gold Glove. Edgar Martinez continued his steady production Mariner fans had come to expect, hitting 23 home runs and driving in 116 while slashing .306/.423/.543.

While this potent line-up stayed busy leading the majors with 927 runs, the pitching staff worked just as hard in holding opponents to an MLB low of 627 scores. Four hurlers in the starting rotation accounted for 56% of the total innings pitched that season and combined for a 70-21 record with a 3.53 ERA. Thirty-eight-year-old Jamie Moyer, with 16 big-league seasons under his belt and another 11 to go before calling it quits, led the staff with 20 wins. Paul Abbott, who left baseball at the age of 25 after throwing only 111 innings over four seasons and compiling a 5.25 ERA, came out of nowhere to post 17 wins. Freddie Garcia, runner-up to Carlos Beltran for the AL Rookie-of-the-Year in 1999, led the AL with a 3.05 ERA and 238 innings pitched, contributing another 18 wins. Aaron Sele rounded out the top four rotation spots with 15 victories. The bullpen proved to be just as stingy, saving 56 of their 73 opportunities, Kazuhiro Sasaki placing second to Mariano Rivera in the AL with 45 saves.

After completing an 8-game win streak on May 17, the Mariners owned 31 victories in their first 40 games of the season and a 12-game lead on the second-place Angels, a lead that would grow at one point to 21 but never diminish to less than 11. They wrapped up another streak in early June, winning 15 consecutive contests to improve their record to 47-12 for an incredible .797 winning percentage. Entering the post-season, they repeated their 2000 feat in winning their AL Division Series, besting the Cleveland Indians three games to two. But facing the Yankees in the ALCS, they went out in five games, becoming arguably the greatest team not to have advanced to the World Series.

Here's a game played on May 16 during that 116-win season against the Chicago White Sox. Typical of their new look, the Mariners relied less on the long ball and more on a balanced line-up that generated ten hits and drew four walks to produce a 7-2 victory in this early season matchup. Paul Abbott took the hill for the home team and scattered three hits over 6.1 innings allowing only two runs. He struck out ten White Sox hitters.

Chicago Whitesox at **Seattle Mariners**

May 16, 2001

Batting	1	2	3	4	5	6	7	8	9	AB	R	H	RBI
Ichiro Suzuki RF										4	0	2	1
Mark McLemore 3B										2	0	1	0
David Bell 3B										3	1	1	1
Edgar Martinez DH										4	0	1	0
John Olerud 1B										4	0	1	2
Bret Boone 2B										4	1	1	0
Mike Cameron CF										2	2	1	0
Stan Javier LF										4	0	0	0
Tom Lampkin C										3	1	0	0
Carlos Guillen SS										3	2	2	3
Runs	0	3	0	0	0	0	2	2	x				
Left on Base													

2B: Ichiro Suzuki (off Rocky Biddle); John Olerud (off Lorenzo Barcelo); Mike Cameron (off Sean Lowe)

SH: Carlos Guillen (off Kelly Wunsch)

HBP: Tom Lampkin (off Kelly Wunsch)

2-Out RBI: Carlos Guillen 3; John Olerud 2; David Bell; Ichiro Suzuki

Team LOB: 8

Reached on FC: David Bell

Hint: The Mariners leave at least one runner on base every inning but two, and those two occurred consecutively.

Pitching	IP	H	R	ER	BB	BF
Rocky Biddle	6	5	3	3	2	25
Kelly Wunsch	0.1	0	2	2	1	3
Lorenzo Barcelo	0.2	1	0	0	1	4
Sean Lowe	1	4	2	2	0	7

SOLUTION   **2001 Seattle Mariners**

Batting	1	2	3	4	5	6	7	8	9	AB	R	H	RBI
Ichiro Suzuki RF	X	H,I			X		W,X	H		4	0	2	1
Mark McLemore 3B	H	X								2	0	1	0
David Bell 3B					X		FC,R	H,I		3	1	1	1
Edgar Martinez DH	X		H		X		W	X		4	0	1	0
John Olerud 1B	X		X			X	H,2I			4	0	1	2
Bret Boone 2B		H,R	X			X	X			4	1	1	0
Mike Cameron CF		W,R	X			W		H,R		2	2	1	0
Stan Javier LF		X		X		X		X		4	0	0	0
Tom Lampkin C		X		X			HBP,R	X		3	1	0	0
Carlos Guillen SS		H,R,2I		X			SH,X	H,R,I		3	2	2	3
Runs	0	3	0	0	0	0	2	2	x				
Left on Base	1	1	1	0	0	1	2	2	x				

With the Mariners having sent 39 hitters to the plate, everyone in the order had four plate appearances except for the top three who each had five. Those charged with fewer at-bats compared to plate appearances, included Guillen with an SH and Lampkin with a HBP as disclosed in the notes, Suzuki and Martinez with a walk, and Cameron with two free passes.

7th Inning

Wunsch came in the game during the 7th and pitched to the 26th, 27th, and 28th hitters: Lampkin, Guillen, and Suzuki. Per the notes, he hit Lampkin with a pitch and then gave up the SH to Guillen.

That leaves Suzuki to have drawn the walk issued by Wunsch.

Barcello then came in to face the next four batters and recorded two outs while giving up a hit and a walk. The fourth and final batter he faced was Boone, so he was out to end the inning.

Per the notes, Olerud doubled off Barcello, so that had to occur this inning, accounting for the one hit.

The walk given up by Barcello had to be to Martinez, as Bell received no walks in the game.

This leaves Bell as the other out recorded by Barcello.

Now looking back to determine who scored during the inning, the first had to have been by Lampkin who led off being hit by a pitch.

Guillen could not have scored, as he was out on the sacrifice. The next runner to reach base was Suzuki, but he scored no runs during the game. In fact, the only remaining batter coming to the plate this inning who scored a run was Bell. For Bell to have scored while also accounting for one of the outs recorded by Wunsch, he had to reach base on the FC disclosed in the notes. Suzuki was forced out on the play.

As for the RBIs, note that all the runs scored by the Mariners in this game were scored with two outs. Therefore, as Olerud is the only hitter this inning who came to bat with two outs and was credited with an RBI, he had to knock in both runs this inning.

8th Inning

Cameron had to collect his double disclosed in the notes, to lead off the inning, as this was his only opportunity in facing Lowe.

Javier had no hits or walks for the game, so he was out.

Lampkin had no hits for the game and his HBP is already recorded, so he was out as well.

Martinez was the 7th and final batter to face Lowe, so he was out to end the inning, but that means the next three batters after Lampkin had to reach base. As Lowe walked no one, they all reached on hits.

The two runs scored had to come from the first two reaching base this inning, Cameron and Guillen, as the FC disclosed in the notes was already accounted for and no one else was retired on the bases.

We will come back to determine who picked up the RBIs.

2nd Inning

The remaining three runs scored by the Mariners all came during this inning. The three unaccounted runs scored belong to Boone, Cameron, and Guillen.

Boone and Guillen had to reach on hits as neither drew a walk during the game.

Cameron's lone hit is already recorded so he had to reach on one of his two walks.

Javier and Lampkin were both out as they have no unrecorded hits or walks. This means Olerud could not have led off this inning as he has no unrecorded hits remaining. If he had come to the plate this inning, his out would not have allowed the inning to extend to Guillen.

Guillen had three RBIs for the game on two hits. His hit in the 8th could have produced one RBI, at most, as there was only one runner on ahead of him. Thus, his remaining two RBIs had to come during this at-bat.

Suzuki had to drive in the other run this inning as no one behind him has an unrecorded RBI. Suzuki's hit had to be the double off Biddle disclosed in the notes which knocked in Guillen.

The Mariners left four runners on base over the 7th and 8th and with Olerud making the final out of the 1st, they will leave one on during that frame. That's five runners left on base in three innings, so only three are left stranded during the 2nd through 6th to reach the Team LOB of 8 disclosed in the notes. If two runners were left on base in the 2nd, that would leave only one runner left on base over the next four innings, meaning, three innings ended with no runners left. But per the hint, there were only two innings in which no runners were left on base. Thus, only one runner could be left in the second, so McLemore was out to end the inning.

Back to the 8th

Guillen got two of his three RBIs during the 2nd. The third had to come in the 8th as that was his only other opportunity to drive in a run. Suzuki's RBI came in the 2nd, so that leaves Bell to have driven in the other run during the 8th.

1st Inning

Suzuki was out, as his two hits and walk were already recorded.

McLemore reached on his lone hit to complete his line.

Martinez was out, as the inning did not extend beyond Olerud as previously determined.

3rd – 6th Inning

Per the clue, over the next four innings, two frames end with one runner on and the other two, which occur consecutively, end with no runners on.

The 3rd and 4th cannot be the two consecutive innings with the bases left empty. If the next six batters, starting with Martinez were retired in order, the 5th inning would bring Guillen, Suzuki, and Bell to the plate. As none of them have any unrecorded hits or walks remaining, they would go down in order and we would have a third inning in a row with no runners left on base.

Likewise, the 5th and 6th could not be the consecutive innings either with no runners left. Lampkin led off the 7th. If the six batters before him were retired in order during the 5th and 6th, that would bring Lampkin, Guillen, and Suzuki to the plate during the 4th. As none of them have an unrecorded walk or hit, all would have been retired, leaving no one on base, leading to a third consecutive inning with no runners left on base. Javier might have led off the 4th, but he has no unrecorded walks or hits either.

So, the two consecutive innings with no runners left on base had to be the 4th and 5th, and one runner was left stranded during the 3rd and 6th.

With no runs scored and one runner left on base, four batters would have come to the plate during the 3rd. Of the four batters due up, only Martinez and Cameron have unrecorded walks or hits. Cameron is the fourth batter of the inning though, and as the inning cannot end on a hit or walk, he had to account for the final out and Martinez had to reach base on a hit and left on base.

The next six batters beginning with Javier in the 5th and ending with Martinez in the 6th were all out as none have any unrecorded hits or walks remaining.

In the 6th, Olerud, Boone, and Javier were all out to complete their lines, with Cameron having reached on a walk to account for the stranded runner.

5. Moneyball – 2002 Oakland A's

Michael Lewis's Moneyball introduced many fans to the concept of applying statistical analytics to baseball, or Sabermetrics. The film highlighted how the small-market Oakland A's relied on previously undervalued or newly-developed metrics to reconstruct their roster after the free agent departures of Jason Giambi, Johnny Damon, and Jason Isringhausen. GM Billy Beane targeted candidates with a high on-base percentage as opposed to focusing on traditional measures such as batting average and RBIs. Beane's unconventional choices of an aging veteran, David Justice, and two relatively unknowns: Scott Hatteberg and Jeremy Giambi (Jason's younger brother), helped propel Oakland to a 20-game win streak and capture the 2002 American League West Division title. The A's squeezed an incredible 103 regular season wins out of a $40 million player payroll whereas the Yankees spent almost three times that amount in securing the same number of victories.

The replacements came as advertised, each reaching base at a clip well above the league average. But the real offensive power came from MVP, Miguel Tejada. He belted more than 30 home runs for the third consecutive year and finished third in the league for both hits (204) and RBIs (131). For the season, he slashed .308/.354/.508 while appearing in all 162 games. Veterans Eric Chavez and Jermaine Dye rounded out the heart of the order and contributed a combined 58 home runs and 195 RBIs.

The film also failed to recognize that the secret to the A's success came not at the plate but on the mound. Oakland had drafted and developed a trio of pitchers who had all joined the big-league club by 2000: Tim Hudson, Mark Mulder, and Barry Zito. During the 2001 season, with all three firmly entrenched in the starting rotation, they combined for 56 wins. The following year, the "Moneyball" season, they eclipsed that combined mark by one victory with Cy Young Award winner, Zito leading the way with 23 wins and posting an ERA of 2.75. Mulder contributed 19 wins with a 3.47 ERA while Hudson earned 15 victories and an ERA of 2.98. In the four seasons in which the Big Three spent the entire year together in the rotation, they accounted for more than 45% of the innings pitched and 50% of the wins. Such production from these three workhorses, who each earned a league-minimum salary, provides a more enlightened explanation of Oakland's success on MLB's third-lowest payroll in 2002. The young guns' total hit to Oakland's budget that year amounted to only $1.97 million. By contrast, New York's big three: Mike Mussina, Roger Clemens, and Andy Pettitte commanded a total cost of $30.8 million for their 44 combined wins.

Here's the game in which the A's won their 14th in a row during that 20-game win streak. Mark Mulder threw for seven innings, giving up seven hits and four earned runs to earn his 16th win of the season. Billy Koch, who came over from the Blue Jays via trade to replace Isringhausen, entered the game in the 9th to sew up the victory and notch the 35th of his 44 saves for the year. David Justice, playing in his final season, led the offense with three hits, including a home run and a double, while driving in three runs. The A's 6-4 victory improved their record to 82-51 and put them 3 games ahead of the 2nd-place Anaheim Angels. Of the next 29 games to end the season, they won 21 and easily wrapped up the Western Division title. Their good fortune ended suddenly, however, when they lost to the Minnesota Twins in five games during the AL Division Series.

Oakland A's at Kansas City Royals

August 27, 2002

Batting	1	2	3	4	5	6	7	8	9	AB	R	H	RBI
Ray Durham DH										5	1	1	1
Terrence Long CF										4	0	2	2
Miguel Tejada SS										4	0	0	0
Eric Chavez 3B										4	1	2	0
Jermaine Dye RF										4	1	1	0
David Justice LF										4	1	3	3
John Mabry 1B										4	1	1	0
Mark Ellis 2B										4	0	1	0
Greg Myers C										3	1	1	0
Runs	0	0	1	1	1	1	1	1	0				
Left on Base													

2B: Jermaine Dye (off Runelvys Hernandez); Terrence Long 2 (off Runelvys Hernandez and Jeremy Affeldt);
   Eric Chavez (off Jeremy Affeldt); David Justice (off Jeremy Affeldt)
HR: Ray Durham (off Runelvys Hernandez); David Justice (off Runelvys Hernandez)
SF: Terrence Long (off Runelvys Hernandez)
2-Out RBI: None
Team LOB: 5
Outfield Assist: Eric Chavez thrown out at 2B; Terrence Long thrown out at 3B
Hint: After Chavez was thrown out at second, the succeeding batter reached on a hit.

Pitching	IP	H	R	ER	BB	BF
Runelvys Hernandez	6	8	4	4	1	26
Jeremy Affeldt	2	4	2	2	0	9
Scott Mullen	1	0	0	0	0	3

SOLUTION   Moneyball – 2002 Oakland A's

Batting	1	2	3	4	5	6	7	8	9	AB	R	H	RBI
Ray Durham DH	X		X		H,R,I		X		X	5	1	1	1
Terrence Long CF	X		SF,I,X		H		H,I,X		X	4	0	2	2
Miguel Tejada SS	X		X		X		X			4	0	0	0
Eric Chavez 3B		X		H,X	X			H,R		4	1	2	0
Jermaine Dye RF		X		H,R		X		X		4	1	1	0
David Justice LF		X		H,I		H,R,I		H,I		4	1	3	3
John Mabry 1B			H,R	X		X		X		4	1	1	0
Mark Ellis 2B			H	X		X		X		4	0	1	0
Greg Myers C			W		X		H,R		X	3	1	1	0
Runs	0	0	1	1	1	1	1	1	0				
Left on Base	0	0	2	1	1	0	0	1	0				

Oakland sent 38 batters to the plate during the game, meaning, each person in the order had four plate appearances, with Durham and Long getting an extra turn. Those charged with fewer at-bats than plate appearances were Long with a SF and Myers who drew the lone walk of the game.

9th Inning

Scott Mullen pitched to the 36th, 37th, and 38th batters of the game without allowing a hit or a walk, so Myers, Durham, and Long were all retired.

8th Inning

Working backward, Ellis was out to end the inning, so that Myers could lead off the 9th.

Mabry had only one hit noted in the box score. This hit was the only time he reached base during the game so it must have coincided with his lone run. As Ellis, who had no RBIs, followed Mabry with the final out of the inning, Mabry could not have scored this inning and was therefore out.

Justice had a double off Affeldt as disclosed in the notes. As this was his only plate appearance versus Affeldt, the double must have occurred at this point.

Jermaine Dye had one hit during the game, but per the notes, that was a double off Hernandez. As Dye had no other hits and no walks during the game, he was out.

Per the notes, Chavez had a double off Affeldt. That may have occurred to end the 7th as the notes also mention that Chavez was thrown out at second base sometime during the game. If that scenario had unfolded, however, there would be no one to account for the one run scored during the 8th. Thus, Chavez doubled off Affeldt here in the 8th and came around to score on the hit by Justice.

7th Inning

Tejada went hitless for the game and had no walks. Thus, he had to account for the final out of the 7th inning. If he had been retired to lead off the 8th, the inning could not have extended to Ellis.

Long doubled in his only opportunity versus Affeldt per the notes, so that had to occur this inning.

Durham's lone hit of the game was a home run off Hernandez, so he was out this inning.

Eight of the nine batters Affeldt faced have been accounted for as well as three of the four hits he allowed. Having worked backward, Myers is now the last hitter to face Affeldt and must have reached base on a hit. Myers also must have scored the run this inning as the only other batter to reach base during the inning was Long, but he was not credited with a run in the box score.

This leaves us with only two outs recorded for the inning, but per the notes, Long was thrown out at 3rd base during the game. That must have occurred this inning while he attempted to stretch his double into a triple.

The only viable candidates for the RBI this inning were Durham and Long, but Durham's RBI would come with his HR, leaving Long as the one who drove Myers home this inning.

1st Inning

Durham's only hit of the game was a home run, and as the A's did not score this inning, the homer did not come at this point. Durham was therefore out.

Tejada went hitless for the game, so he was out as well.

2nd Inning

The 1st inning may have extended to Chavez if Long reached base on the first of his two hits. But the inning could not have extended beyond Chavez, as he has only one hit remaining and per the notes, he was subsequently thrown out after reaching on that hit. Thus, Dye had to come to the plate during the 2nd.

Dye has an unrecorded hit and run scored. Those had to occur together and as the A's failed to score this inning, Dye was retired.

Note the A's score no more than one run in any inning. This means Justice can pick up only one RBI at a time. With his three hits matching his three RBIs, his hits must come during those innings in which the A's score. With no runs scored here in the 2nd, Justice was out.

3rd Inning

At this point, two of the six RBIs are accounted for. Two of the four unrecorded RBIs belong to Justice. With the A's scoring only one run in the 3rd, and Justice having batted during the 2nd, there is no plausible scenario for him to collect an RBI this inning. That leaves either Durham or Long to drive in the run this frame.

Durham did have a home run off Hernandez that is not yet recorded. Mabry and Ellis might have reached base on hits in the 2nd. Myers could have then ended the inning and allowed Durham to lead off the 3rd with a solo home run to account for the one run scored in the inning. But Mabry scores a run at some point in the game and thus had to reach base on his lone hit during an inning in which the A's scored. So, if Mabry did come to the plate in the 2nd, he was out. That would leave Ellis and Myers to lead off the 3rd, and both would have had to have been out so as not to score on Durham's HR. But the A's had no 2-Out RBIs during the game, so this scenario is not plausible either.

That leaves Long as the only possibility for the RBI this inning. Of the hitters in front of Long, Mabry is the only one with an unrecorded run, so he must have reached base on his hit. Myers's run scored was already accounted for and Durham's will come on his home run.

Durham was out as his only hit was a home run.

Note that Long has a Sacrifice Fly. As his other RBI has already been recorded, his RBI here in the 2nd had to come via the SF. His double off Hernandez must have occurred at some other time in the game.

There had to have been less than two outs for Long to be credited with an SF. Hence, both Ellis and Myers had to reach base safely, Ellis by his lone hit of the game, and Myers by a walk as his hit is already recorded.

Tejada, once again, made the final out of the inning, as he had no hits or walks for the game.

Back to the 1st and 2nd Innings

Chavez had to account for one of the outs during the 2nd as only three batters came to the plate. He might have led off with a hit and then subsequently been thrown out at second per the notes, but even so, he had to account for one of the outs.

Long had to account for the second out of the 1st as the frame did not extend beyond Tejada.

4th Inning

Like his at-bat in the 2nd, even if Chavez collected the first of his two hits here, he was thrown out at second per the notes, so he had to account for one of the outs this frame.

Only Justice and Durham have RBIs to still record. Justice had to collect one of his two remaining RBIs this inning as the order cannot get back around to Durham with less than two outs and no runs scored. Justice might have hit his HR during the inning, but as the A's scored only one run, that would mean Dye had to have been retired for the second out of the inning. As there were no 2-out RBIs, however, Dye had to reach safely and then come around to score on one of Justice's three hits. The only means Dye had of reaching base was his double off Hernandez.

Mabry and Ellis were both retired to end the inning as neither has any unrecorded hits or walks remaining.

5th Inning

Myers led off the inning with an out to complete his line.

Durham hit his home run this inning to complete his line and account for the one run scored this inning.

Long reached on his double off Hernandez to complete his line.

Tejada was out to complete his hitless game.

Like his at-bats in the 2nd and 4th, Chavez might have reached on the first of his two hits but as he was thrown out at second per the notes, he had to account for the final out of this frame.

6th Inning

Dye was out to complete his line.

Justice hit his home run to complete his line.

Both Mabry and Ellis were retired to complete their lines.

Chavez

Relying on the hint disclosed in the notes, Chavez was thrown out a second in the 4th inning as Dye followed up with a base hit.

6. Hank Greenberg

Hank Greenberg's final season of his hall-of-fame career coincided with that of another future inductee's inaugural year. They met as opponents during an early season matchup in 1947 and collided during a play at first base. After assuring the rookie was unharmed, Greenberg offered these words of encouragement to Jackie Robinson, "Stick in there. You're doing fine. Keep your chin up." As a Jewish ballplayer, Greenberg faced antisemitism throughout his career and empathized with Robinson and the racial malice directed his way. Like Robinson, he faced bigoted insults hurled from the grandstands and the bench jockeying of opposing dugouts. They even shared a common nemesis in Ben Chapman, the infamous manager of the Philadelphia Phillies whose disgraceful taunting of Robinson led to a well-publicized and forced conciliatory photo-op.

While Greenberg showed less restraint than Robinson in his response to the vile behavior, he, too, used his bat as the primary weapon in delivering vengeance. With his powerful 6' 3," 210 lb. frame, he quickly developed into one of the game's greatest right-handed hitters. By his second full season with the Tigers, he set a high standard that he would follow for seven consecutive seasons: a batting average above .300, an on-base percentage exceeding .400, and a lofty slugging percentage of at least .600. In three of those campaigns, he led all baseball in RBIs and in 1937, fell seven shy of Hack Wilson's record of 191. He also chased Babe Ruth's single-season record of 60 home runs when he clouted 58 round-trippers in 1938. Twice more during that seven-year stretch, he led the AL in homers.

His offensive production earned MVP Awards in 1935 and again in 1940, but also helped propel the Tigers back into the postseason for the first time in 25 years. With Greenberg joining veterans Mickey Cochran and Charlie Gehringer, the Tigers won the AL pennant in 1934 with 101 regular season wins before falling to the St. Louis Cardinals in the World Series. Undaunted, the Tigers again took the pennant the following year and finally laid claim to the franchise's first World Series title. Detroit advanced to two more World Series during Greenberg's tenure, losing in 1940, but winning their second title in 1945.

Military service kept Greenberg away from the baseball diamond for all but 97 games between those last two World Series appearances. On May 6, 1941, he homered twice off the Yankees and then departed for Fort Custer, Michigan as part of an infantry unit after his draft number had come up. Shortly thereafter, Congress passed a law exempting anyone over the age of 28 from the draft and thus 30-year-old Greenberg received an honorable discharge on December 5. Two days later, the bombing of Pearl Harbor led him to voluntarily enlist in the US Army Air Forces where he served for three years. In his first game back, on July 1, 1945, he once again homered. An even greater gift to the Detroit fans came during the last game of the regular season when Greenberg clinched the pennant with a ninth-inning grand slam.

In his first full season back from war, Greenberg quickly regained form, slugging over .600 and once again leading the league in home runs and RBIs. Despite such production, Tigers' owner Walter Briggs unceremoniously released Greenberg and assigned his contract to the Pirates. After one year in Pittsburgh, Greenberg retired with a career slash line of .313/.412/.605. His OPS of 1.017 still ranks 6th of all time.

Here's a game from the 1935 season in which Greenberg won the first of his two MVP Awards. Greenberg, along with fellow Hall of Famers, Mickey Cochrane and Charlie Gehringer each contributed a home run and two hits as the Tigers put up 9 runs against their hosts, the Chicago White Sox. General Crowder started for the Tigers and went seven innings, giving up only two runs on four hits and four walks to earn his eighth victory of the season. Schoolboy Rowe, who started the prior game for the Tigers, finished the last two innings, allowing only one hit and no runs to pick up the save.

Detroit Tigers at Chicago White Sox
June 27, 1935

Batting	1	2	3	4	5	6	7	8	9	AB	R	H	RBI
Pete Fox RF										4	2	2	2
Mickey Cochrane C										5	2	2	1
Charlie Gehringer 2B										4	1	2	2
Hank Greenberg 1B										4	2	2	2
Goose Goslin LF										4	0	1	1
Billy Rogell SS										4	0	1	0
Gee Walker CF										4	0	1	1
Marv Owen 3B										4	0	0	0
General Crowder P										3	1	1	0
Schoolboy Rowe P										1	1	1	0
Runs	2	2	2	0	0	0	1	1	1				
Left on Base													

2B: Hank Greenberg (off Vern Kennedy); Billy Rogell (off Carl Fischer)

HR: Pete Fox (off Vern Kennedy); Charlie Gehringer (off Vern Kennedy); Mickey Cochrane (off Carl Fischer); Hank Greenberg (off Carl Fischer)

SH: Charlie Gehringer (off Vern Kennedy); Pete Fox (off Sad Sam Jones)

*SF: Hank Greenberg (off Vern Kennedy)

2-Out RBI: Pete Fox 2; Charlie Gehringer; Mickey Cochrane; Gee Walker; Goose Goslin

Team LOB: 4

Reached on Error: Pete Fox

Runners retired on the bases: Gee Walker picked off by Vern Kennedy

Pitching	IP	H	R	ER	BB	BF
Vern Kennedy	3	8	6	6	0	16
Carl Fischer	5	3	2	2	0	19
Sad Sam Jones	1	2	1	1	0	5

SOLUTION   Hank Greenberg

Batting	1	2	3	4	5	6	7	8	9	AB	R	H	RBI
Peter Fox RF	H,R	H,R,2I		E			X		SH,X	4	2	2	2
Mickey Cochrane C	H,R	X		X			H,R,I		X	5	2	2	1
Charlie Gehringer 2B	SH,X		H,R,I		X		X		H,I	4	1	2	2
Hank Greenberg 1B	SF,I,X		H,R		X			H,R,I	X	4	2	2	2
Goose Goslin LF	H,I		X		X			X		4	0	1	1
Billy Rogell SS	X		X			X		H		4	0	1	0
Gee Walker CF		X	H,I,X			X		X		4	0	1	1
Marv Owen 3B		X		X		X		X		4	0	0	0
General Crowder P		H,R		X			X			3	1	1	0
Schoolboy Rowe P									H,R	1	1	1	0
Runs	2	2	2	0	0	0	1	1	1				
Left on Base	1	0	0	1	0	0	0	1	1				

Having sent 40 batters to the plate during the game, the first four positions in the Tigers' line-up had five plate appearances, while the bottom five had only four. Those charged with fewer at-bats than plate appearances were Gehringer and Fox each with an SH and Greenberg with a SF.

9th Inning

The 40th and final batter of the game for the Tigers was Greenberg, so he was out to end the 9th.

Per the notes, Pete Fox had an SH off Jones, and as this was Jones's only inning of work, the SH must have occurred during this plate appearance.

Schoolboy Rowe entered the 9th to replace Crowder. As this was his only at-bat during the game, he must have picked up his hit and run scored during this inning.

Of the remaining two batters Jones faced: Fox and Gehringer, one had to account for the second out of the inning and the other drove in Rowe. Per the notes, Cochrane had a home run off Fischer at some point in the game which would account for his RBI, so Gehringer must have driven in the run with a hit while Cochrane was out.

4th – 8th Innings

Marv Owen was the last batter to face Carl Fischer, so he was out to end the 8th.

Fischer pitched five innings, from the 4th to the 8th, giving up single runs in the 7th and 8th. He also served up two home runs, meaning each was a solo shot: one to Cochrane and one to Greenberg. Note that Cochrane's lone RBI, which resulted from the HR, came with two outs. For him to have slugged the round-tripper in the 8th, the next five batters would have had to reach base safely to extend the inning to Owen for the final out, without scoring an additional run. As this was not plausible, Cochrane had to notch his dinger in the 7th while Greenberg got his in the 8th.

The only other hit Fischer allowed was the double to Rogell, which must have occurred in the 8th to extend the inning to Owen.

Now that all three hits allowed by Fischer are recorded, everyone else facing him during his five innings of work was out except for Fox. Looking at Fischer's line, he pitched five full innings equating to 15 outs, and allowed three hits, for a total of 18 batters. He faced 19 batters in total, however, meaning someone reached base by means other than a hit or walk. Per the notes, Fox reached on an error at some point in the game, so that had to occur while Fischer was on the mound. Fox could not have reached base in front of Cochrane's homer in the 7th as that was a solo shot.

Going to the 4th inning when Fischer came into the game, the first batter he faced was the 17th hitter in the line-up: Owen. Again, as all three hits allowed by Fischer are already recorded, Owen was out, as was Crowder.

Fox was next, and as this was his only other opportunity to face Fischer, he had to reach on the error at this point.

Every remaining batter Fischer faced from the 4th through 8th inning was retired.

1st Inning

Fox has two at-bats remaining and reached base on both. One of these was a home run, but as both of Fox's RBIs came with 2 outs, the HR could not have occurred during the 1st. Hence, Fox led off the game with a single.

Gehringer also has two remaining at-bats, one resulted in an SH and the other an HR. Gehringer had two RBIs during the game, but one of those was already recorded, meaning his HR had to be a solo shot. With Fox already on base, Gehringer's homer must come later, leaving this at-bat for the SH.

The candidates for the two RBIs this inning are now whittled down to Greenberg, Goslin, and Walker. If the inning extended to Walker, there would be two outs as the batter in front of him, Rogell, had his lone hit already recorded. But as Walker had no 2-out RBIs, he can be ruled out, leaving Greenberg and Goslin to have picked up the RBIs.

Greenberg does have an unrecorded hit, but per the notes, he picked up one of his RBIs with an SF. As his other RBI was already recorded, this one had to come via the SF, scoring Fox.

Cochrane had to reach base, as there had to be fewer than two outs for Greenberg's SF. Thus, Cochrane reached on one of his two hits.

Goslin, as established above, picked up the other RBI this inning, doing so with his lone hit and driving in Cochrane.

Rogell, as mentioned above, was out, as his lone hit was already recorded.

2nd Inning

Walker's hit must have been reserved for his RBI, so he led off this inning with an out.

Owen was hitless for the game, so he too was out.

Crowder had to reach base with a hit and score to complete his line.

Fox hit his home run off Kennedy and picked up two RBIs to complete his line.

Cochrane was out to complete his line.

3rd Inning

Gehringer led off the inning with his HR off Kennedy to complete his line.

Greenberg collected his double off Kennedy and then scored this inning to complete his line.

Goslin and Rogell were both out to complete their lines.

Walker collected his hit and RBI to complete his line but had to be picked off by Kennedy, per the notes, to end the inning, so that Owen could lead off the 3rd.

7. Harmon Killebrew

Harmon Killebrew began his MLB career in 1954 as a highly touted bonus baby with the Washington Senators. The size of the contract required the 17-year-old's inclusion on the major league roster for two years. Though used sparingly during those early years and eventually spending some time in the minors, Killebrew earned his way into the starting line-up by 1959 and remained at the heart of the Senator's/Twin's batting order for the next 14 years.

He cemented himself as one of the game's most prolific sluggers with the frequency and distance of his home runs. He led the American League in round-trippers six times and finished in the top five on 12 occasions. By the time he hung up his spikes after the 1975 season, he had slugged 573 home runs, putting him in fifth place on the career list at the time behind Ruth, Aaron, Mays, and Frank Robinson. Today, he sits at 12th. Measured in terms of at-bats per home run, Killebrew ranks as the 7th most productive hitter in baseball history, knocking one over the wall every 14.2 trips to the plate. His prodigious strength is best memorialized by a plaque at Mall of America in Minnesota, the former site of the Metropolitan Stadium, which marks the landing spot of his 522-foot shot in 1967.

Killebrew's lone MVP came in 1969 when he led the Twins to 97 wins and a division title with 49 home runs, 140 RBIs with a 1.011 OPS. The season was hardly an outlier though as he averaged 38 homers and 105 RBIs a season. He finished in the top 15 for the MVP in nine other seasons and was selected as an all-star eleven times.

It took four ballots before Killebrew gained entrance into the MLB Hall of Fame, many feeling his .256 batting average and high strike-out total delayed his enshrinement. But perhaps Killebrew was just ahead of his time. When reflecting on his career, he told author Danny Peary of We Played the Game, "I think I could have been a .300 hitter, but I decided early on that I was helping the club more by driving in a lot of runs than going for a high average." Music to the ears of modern-day Bill James disciples who would have glossed over the batting average and whiffs, focusing instead on the career .376 on-base percentage and .509 slugging.

Here's a game from that MVP season in which Killebrew homered twice and drove in three runs as the Twins defeated the Cleveland Indians 10-3. Fellow Hall-of-Famers Rod Carew and Tony Oliva each chipped in two hits apiece. Jim Kaat already in his 11th of 25 big-league seasons and another future Hall -of-Famer, took the mound for the Twins and outdueled Luis Tiant for his second win of the young season. He went the full distance, giving up eight hits and two walks. The win put the Twins 1.5 games ahead of Oakland, whom they battled for the American League West lead during the early season. But after a three-game sweep of the A's over the 4th of July weekend, the Twins never looked back and clinched the division title by nine games. Unfortunately, they faced a pitching staff of Cuellar, McNally, and Palmer in the AL Championship Series which saw Baltimore sweep the Twins in three games.

Minnesota Twins at Cleveland Indians

May 7, 1969

Batting	1	2	3	4	5	6	7	8	9	AB	R	H	RBI
Ted Uhlaender CF										5	2	1	2
Rod Carew 2B										5	0	2	1
Tony Oliva RF										4	1	2	2
Harmon Killebrew 3B										4	2	2	3
Charlie Manuel LF										3	1	1	0
Cesar Tovar LF										1	0	0	0
Rich Reese 1B										5	1	1	0
Leo Cardenas SS										4	1	0	0
John Roseboro C										4	2	0	0
Jim Kaat P										4	0	2	2
Runs	0	3	0	0	3	4	0	0	0				
Left on Base													

2B: Jim Kaat (off Luis Tiant); Rich Reese (off Mike Paul)

HR: Harmon Killebrew 2 (both off Luis Tiant)

2-Out RBI: Jim Kaat 2; Harmon Killebrew 2; Tony Oliva

Team LOB: 7

Reached on Error: John Roseboro

Reached on FC: Ted Uhlaender

Hint: Manuel reached on a walk before his base hit.

Pitching	IP	H	R	ER	BB	BF
Luis Tiant	5	6	6	4	1	23
Mike Paul	0.1	4	4	4	2	7
Stan Williams	1.2	0	0	0	0	5
Juan Pizarro	1	1	0	0	2	6
Gary Kroll	1	0	0	0	0	3

SOLUTION   Harmon Killebrew

Batting	1	2	3	4	5	6	7	8	9	AB	R	H	RBI
Ted Uhlaender CF	X	X			FC,R	H,R,2I		X		5	2	1	2
Rod Carew 2B	X		X		X	H,I		H		5	0	2	1
Tony Oliva RF	X		X		H,R,I	H,I		W		4	1	2	2
Harmon Killebrew 3B		H,R,I	X		H,R,2I	X		W		4	2	2	3
Charlie Manuel LF		W,R		H	X	X				3	1	1	0
Cesar Tovar LF								X		1	0	0	0
Rich Reese 1B		X		X		H,R	X		X	5	1	1	0
Leo Cardenas SS		X		X		W,R	X		X	4	1	0	0
John Roseboro C		E,R		X		W,R	X		X	4	2	0	0
Jim Kaat P		H,2I			H,X	X		X		4	0	2	2
Runs	0	3	0	0	3	4	0	0	0				
Left on Base	0	1	0	1	0	2	0	3	0				

The Twins sent a total of 44 batters to the plate during the game, which means each position in the line-up, except for the last, had five plate appearances. Those, other than Kaat, charged with less than five at-bats were Oliva, Killebrew, Manuel/Tovar, Cardenas, and Roseboro, each having drawn a walk.

9th Inning

Gary Kroll pitched to the last three hitters of the game, starting with the 42nd batter, Rich Reese, and retired each of them as he gave up no hits or walks.

8th Inning

Tovar was the final batter to face Pizarro, so he ended the inning with an out.

Of the five batters preceding Tovar to the plate this inning, two received walks. As Oliva and Killebrew were the only two of those five to have drawn a walk during the game, they each reached on a free pass this inning.

6th and 7th Innings

Stan Williams came in during the 6th with one out to face the 31st batter of the game. He retired all five batters he faced, two to end the 6th, beginning with Killebrew, and three during the 7th, ending with Roseboro.

Reese was the 24th batter of the game for the Twins and the first to face Mike Pau while leading off the 6th. Per the notes, he greeted Reese with a double.

The Twins put up four runs during the inning. Of the batters preceding Killebrew's second out of the inning, five have unrecorded runs scored. Oliva is one of these, but as there is no one behind him to bring him home, that leaves Reese, Cardenas, Roseboro, and Uhlaender as the run scorers during the 6th.

Paul walked two of the seven batters he faced. Of those seven, Cardenas and Roseboro are the only two at this point with unrecorded walks so they had to reach on the free passes in the 6th.

With the double and two walks prior to his at-bat, Kaat came to the plate during the 6th, with bases loaded and no outs. Any hit by Kaat, at this point, was sure to drive in a run, but both of Kaat's RBIs for the game came with two outs. Kaat, therefore, accounted for the first out of the inning.

That leaves the top three in the order to drive in the four runs scored during the inning. At most, Oliva could only drive in one as one of his RBIs came with two outs and another came with less than two outs. Carew only had one RBI for the game, so the only plausible scenario was Uhlaender drove in two, Carew one, and Oliva one.

For Uhlaender to drive in two, he had to reach on his hit, and not the FC. Carew and Oliva, likewise, had to reach on base-hits as neither had an unrecorded walk.

5th Inning

Manuel was out to end the 5th as he was the 23rd and final batter to face Tiant.

Killebrew's two home runs had to occur in the 2nd and 5th, as those are the only two remaining innings in which the Twins scored. For Killebrew to come to the plate during the 2nd, the top three in the order had to be retired in the 1st. As the HR in the 2nd was a lead-off solo shot, the homer in the 5th had to account for the other two RBIs, as Killebrew had no other hits during the game. These two RBIs came with two outs per the notes.

Carew had to account for one of the outs during the inning, otherwise, he would have scored on Killebrew's HR.

If Kaat came to bat this inning, there could not have been two out while he was at the plate. As both his RBIs came with two out, it was not plausible for him to have driven home a run this inning, leaving Oliva to record his 2-out RBI this frame, after reaching on a base hit and then scoring on Killebrew's HR.

Roseboro still has an unrecorded run, but for him to score the one remaining run this inning, both Kaat and Uhlaender would have had to be out so as not to also score. But that scenario would not have allowed the inning to extend to Manuel for the final out. Thus, Uhlaender scored the first run of the inning. As his hit is already recorded, Uhlaender must have reached on the FC this inning.

Kaat had to reach on one of his base hits to put Uhlaender's FC in order but was then forced out so as not to score.

2nd Inning

As already mentioned above, Killebrew led off the inning with an HR.

The two remaining unrecorded runs belong to Manuel and Roseboro, so each reached base this inning and eventually scored.

Per the hint, Manuel reached base by the walk prior to his hit, so the free pass occurred this at-bat.

Roseboro's walk was already recorded and as he had no hits during the game, he must have reached on the error disclosed in the notes.

The only two remaining RBIs belong to Kaat, so he had to reach base this inning, likely with the double off Tiant disclosed in the notes, driving in both Manuel and Roseboro. As the RBIs came with two outs, both Reese and Cardenas had to be out before Kaat's at-bat.

Uhlaender was out to end the inning as his hit was already recorded.

Back to the 8th

With Kaat's two hits now recorded, he had to start the 8th with an out.

Uhlaender was out as well as his hit was already recorded.

That leaves Carew as the one to have picked up the lone hit allowed by Pizzaro and extend the inning.

Manuel has the only remaining unrecorded hit. Hence, Tiant retired the side in order during both the 1st and 3rd innings. Manuel then led off the 4th with his hit followed by three outs to end the inning.

8. The Miracle Mets – 1969 New York Mets

Even before the Dodgers and Giants departed for the west coast to begin the 1958 season, the city of New York began its quest for a National League replacement. Informed of MLB owners' unanimous consent to allow the two teams to relocate, Mayor Robert Wagner tapped William Shea in November of 1957 to head the efforts in securing a senior-circuit franchise for the Big Apple. After giving up on the idea of convincing any existing clubs to relocate, Shea teamed up with Branch Rickey in threatening the development of a rival league. Only then did MLB finally acquiesce to the idea of expansion, awarding New York and Houston teams in the National League, while LA and Minneapolis gained entry into the American League.

The National League owners quickly extracted a modicum of revenge upon the gatecrashers, however, in concocting rules of an expansion draft that served to line their own pockets while assuring a dismal start for the newcomers. In conducting the expansion draft prior to the annual Rule 5 draft, any young, promising minor leaguers were off-limits to the Mets and Colt 45s, leaving them to sort through the rubbish of aging veterans, journeymen, and utility players. Don Zimmer led the Met's draft class in clouting 13 home runs and driving in 40 runs during the preceding season, while pitcher Roger Craig's 5 wins topped all his fellow draft mates. Armed with such a feckless roster, manager, Casey Stengel led his charges to a record of futility during that inaugural 1962 season, winning only 40 of their 162 games.

In 1967, the Mets finished with over 100 losses for the fifth time in their six-year history, but the cornerstone for future success had been laid. Tom Seaver, who spent only one year down in the minors, joined the opening-day roster that season and went on to win 16 games for a team that earned only 61 victories. His 2.76 ERA and 170 strikeouts easily garnered the NL Rookie of the Year Award. Jerry Koosman joined the starting rotation later that year, appearing in only three games, but picked up 19 wins the following season on his way to finishing second in the Rookie of the Year balloting.

With Seaver and Koosman anchoring a dominant pitching staff, the Mets went on to shock the world of baseball in 1969. Not only did they post their first winning season, but they completely flipped the script in winning 100 games. They easily captured the NL East Division, besting the second-place Cubs by eight games, and then swept the Atlanta Brave in three games, to earn their spot in the World Series where they defeated the Baltimore Orioles four games to one.

Seaver led the entire league with 25 wins during that championship season, posting a 2.21 ERA and striking out 208 during his 273.1 innings pitched. He easily captured the NL Cy Young Award and nearly took home the MVP Award as well, finishing a close second behind Willie McCovey. Koosman added another 17 wins while throwing 241 innings with a 2.28 ERA. Nolan Ryan, limited to only 25 appearances because of his Army Reserve requirement, also picked up six wins, striking out 92 hitters in only 89.1 innings of work. While the starters completed 51 games, Tug McGraw made 42 appearances mostly out of the pen and collected 9 wins and 12 saves.

Tommy Agee's 26 home runs and Cleon Jones's .340 batting average led the Mets' attack. Yet, despite the two outfielders placing 6th and 7th, respectively, amongst the NL MVP candidates, the offense proved rather anemic in producing only 3.90 runs a game versus a league average of 4.05. But with the pitching staff holding opponents to only 3.34 runs a game, manager Gil Hodges's lineup more than rose to the occasion.

Here's a game from that 1969 championship season in which Seaver started and finished en route to a 7-3 victory over the visiting Pittsburg Pirates. He held Roberto Clemente hitless in his four plate appearances, striking him out twice. Overall, Tom Terrific gave up six hits and walked four while striking out ten to pick up his 12th victory of the year. The win put the Mets at 39-32, 8.5 games behind the 1st-place Cubs. By August 13, that deficit had increased to 10 games, but the Miracle Mets won 38 of their final 49 games to secure the division crown.

Pittsburgh Pirates at **New York Mets**
       June 29, 1969

Batting	1	2	3	4	5	6	7	8	9	AB	R	H	RBI
Rod Gaspar RF										5	0	0	0
Bobby Pfeil 2B										5	0	2	0
Tommie Agee CF										3	2	1	0
Cleon Jones LF										3	3	1	2
Ed Charles 3B										4	1	3	2
Donn Clendenon 1B										4	0	2	3
Jerry Grote C										4	0	1	0
Al Weis SS										2	0	0	0
Wayne Garrett SS										1	0	0	0
Tom Seaver P										4	1	1	0
Runs	2	0	2	3	0	0	0	0	x				
Left on Base													

2B: Ed Charles (off Bob Veale); Donn Clendenon (off Bob Veale);Tom Seaver (off Bob Veale)
3B: Cleon Jones (off Bob Veale)
2-Out RBI: Ed Charles 2; Cleon Jones 2; Donn Clendenon
Team LOB: 8
Reached on FC: Cleon Jones
Hint: Agee reached on a hit before his two walks.

Pitching	IP	H	R	ER	BB	BF
Bob Veale	3.2	7	7	7	4	22
Bruce Dal Canton	2.1	2	0	0	0	9
Chuck Hartenstein	2	2	0	0	0	8

SOLUTION   **The Miracle Mets – 1969 New York Mets**

Batting	1	2	3	4	5	6	7	8	9	AB	R	H	RBI
Rod Gaspar RF	X	X		X		X		X		5	0	0	0
Bobby Pfeil 2B	X	X		X		H		H		5	0	2	0
Tommie Agee CF	H,R		W,X	W,R		X		X		3	2	1	0
Cleon Jones LF	W,R		FC,R	H,R,2I		X				3	3	1	2
Ed Charles 3B	H,I		H,R	H,I			X			4	1	3	2
Donn Clendenon 1B	H,I		H,2I	X			X			4	0	2	3
Jerry Grote C	X		X		X		H			4	0	1	0
Al Weis SS		W	X		X					2	0	0	0
Wayne Garrett SS							X			1	0	0	0
Tom Seaver P		X		H,R	X			X		4	1	1	0
Runs	2	0	2	3	0	0	0	0	x				
Left on Base	2	1	1	1	0	1	1	1	x				

With the Mets having sent a total of 39 batters to the plate during the game, each position in the order stepped into the batter's box four times, with the top three getting a fifth opportunity. Those charged with fewer at-bats than plate appearances were Tommie Agee with two walks and Cleon Jones, and the 8th position drawing the other free passes.

4th Inning

Cleon Jones was the 22nd batter of the game for the Mets, and the last to face Veale in the 4th inning. As all seven runs scored by the Mets during the game were charged to Veale, each of the three runs scored during the 4th belonged to him. With Ed Charles facing Dal Canton this inning, he can be ruled out as one of those to have scored this inning, leaving Jones, Seaver, and Agee to account for the three runs.

Seaver had to reach on his only hit for the game, and per the notes, it was a double off Veale.

Agee reached on a walk or hit, which we will come back to. Likewise, we are not certain at this time how Jones reached, whether it was by his hit, walk, or FC.

Gaspar had to account for one of the outs during the inning as he had no hits or walks for the game.

As Pfeil was not credited with any runs scored, he must have been retired prior to Agee scoring. He may have reached base and then forced out on Jones FC, but, nonetheless, accounted for one of the two outs recorded by Veale this inning.

Charles had to reach base this inning on a hit to either drive Jones home, or if nothing more, to at least extend the inning to Clendenon, so that he could drive in the final run of the inning.

1st Inning

Gaspar led off the game with an out as he went hitless for the game.

Jones scored three runs in the game. As the Mets failed to score enough runs in any one inning to allow someone to score twice in one frame, Jones had to score during each of the three innings in which the Mets posted a run. Thus, he had to reach base somehow this inning before coming around to score.

Like the 4th inning, as Pfeil had no runs scored during the game, he must have been retired this inning so as not to score ahead of Jones. He may have reached on one of his two hits and then erased as part of Jones's FC, but in any event, he had to account for one of the outs this inning.

With two outs now recorded, Agee had to reach base to extend the inning. Per the hint, he reached on his lone hit before drawing his two walks. As he was on base in front of Jones, he had to account for the first run scored this inning.

For Jones to score, Charles had to reach base on one of his three hits this inning. Charles's hit may have driven home one or both runs, but at the very least would have served to extend the inning to Clendenon for him to pick up the RBIs.

3rd Inning

As mentioned above, Jones had to cross the plate in each of the three innings the Met scored, so he reached base once again before coming around to score.

Charles owns the only unrecorded run, so he had to score the second run of the 3rd after reaching on one of his three hits.

Clendenon had to follow up with another hit and pick up at least one RBI as no one behind him drove in any runs.

Agee has two unrecorded walks remaining and both came against Veale as the other hurlers gave away no free passes. Agee collected his hit during the 1st, so going back to the 4th, he had to reach on one of the walks during that at-bat. He could not have ended the 2nd with a walk as Jones came to bat during the 3rd. Hence, Agee's first walk had to occur during the 3rd. The two runs the Mets scored this inning were already recorded so Agee must have been erased after reaching base. Hence, Jones hit into the FC this inning before scoring and forced out Agee.

Note that Clendenon had only one 2-out RBI during the game. Based on how the 1st and 4th innings have played out thus far if Clendenon collects an RBI during either of those innings, it will account for that lone 2-out RBI. Thus, his two remaining RBIs, those with one out or less, both had to come here in the 3rd.

Grote and Weis were both retired so that Seaver was able to lead off the 4th.

2nd Inning

Pfeil made the final out of the inning so that Agee could lead off the 3rd.

Gaspar and Seaver were both out as neither have any unrecorded hits or walks remaining.

Weis faced Veale two times and received a walk during one of those appearances. As the second at-bat versus Veale resulted in an out during the 3rd, the walk had to come during his first plate appearance. The 1st inning could not have ended with a walk, so the free pass came here in the 2nd.

Back to the 1st and 4th Innings

Jones reached base in both these innings, once on a triple per the notes, and the other on a walk. If he had tripled during the 1st, that would have produced one RBI and left him with the walk during the 4th. A walk during that inning, however, would not have been enough to produce Jones's second RBI, thus making this scenario implausible. Instead, Jones had to triple during the 4th, picking up his two RBIs and drawing the walk during the 1st.

With Jones on third base with the triple, Charles's hit during the 4th would have easily driven Jones home.

With Charles and Clendenon each having only one unrecorded RBI remaining, they each had to drive home a run during the 1st on base-hits.

Grote was retired to end the 1st so that Weis could lead off the 2nd.

Clendenon was retired to end the 4th as his two hits are now recorded.

7th and 8th Innings

Hartenstein came in to pitch the 7th and 8th innings, throwing to eight batters and allowing only two hits. Of those eight batters he faced, only two have unrecorded hits remaining: Pfeil and Grote. So, starting with the first batter he threw to, the 32nd in the order, Charles, was out.

Clendenon was out as well.

Grote followed with a hit before Garrett ended the inning with an out.

In the 8th inning, Seaver, Gaspar, and Agee were all retired while Pfeil collected his hit.

5th and 6th Innings

Dal Canton came in to finish the 4th and then completed two more frames. During his 2.1 innings pitched, he gave up only two hits, one of which was already recorded, the hit by Charles in the 4th. The only unrecorded hit belongs to Pfeil, so Grote, Weis, and Seaver were set down in order during the 5th.

Gaspar, Agee, and Jones accounted for the three outs in the 6th while Pfeil once again picked up a hit.

9.   Shoeless Joe Jackson

George Landry of the Columbus Ledger-Inquirer once wrote, "Chances are people will talk and wonder about Shoeless Joe Jackson as long as kids grow up with a ball and bat in their hands or grown-ups will fill their favorite bleacher seats at baseball games." With more than a century passing since Jackson's last major league at-bat, time has done little to refute Landry's assertion. Fans, to this day, continue to mythicize the origins of his nickname, revere his career .356 batting average, and of course debate his complicity in fixing the 1919 World Series.

The journey to immortality began in upstate South Carolina where Jackson first starred as a member of a local textile mill squad. Armed with the fabled "Black Betsy," a 36-inch, 48-ounce black-dyed bat, Jackson's display of power and a lofty batting average during his trek through a series of semi-pro and minor league teams earned him a promotion to the big leagues in 1908 with the Philadelphia Athletics. Sensing the need for additional experience and maturity, manager Connie Mack penciled Jackson into the Athletics line-up on only ten occasions during those first two years of pro ball, relegating him to the minors for much of that time. When Mack grew impatient with his young phenom, he traded Jackson away to the Cleveland Naps.

Jackson introduced himself to Cleveland with a .387 average and .587 slugging percentage during the final 20 games of the 1910 season but became a national sensation the following year during his first full year in the majors. He set rookie marks with a .408 batting average which remains untouched and 233 hits which stood until Ichiro Suzuki surpassed him with 242 in 2001. He followed up with an impressive sophomore campaign, leading the majors with 226 hits and 331 total bases, but his .395 average once again failed to top Ty Cobb for the batting title, a disappointment that would recur throughout his career.

In 1913, Jackson again led all of baseball with 197 hits, topped the AL with a .551 slugging percentage, and placed 2nd in voting for the Chalmers Award, a precursor to the MVP honor. But while Jackson continued to battle for a batting title, the Naps slid to the bottom of the AL standings leading to depressed attendance. The resulting financial hit to owner Charley Somers led to a trade of Jackson to the Chicago White Sox midway through the 1915 season.

Jackson continued to add to his impressive resume while with the Sox and in 1917 helped carry Chicago to its first World Series title in eleven seasons. He missed all but 18 games the following season when he opted to work in a shipyard rather than subject himself to military conscription, and the Sox sank to a 6th place finish. But upon his return for the 1919 season, Jackson's .351 average from the clean-up spot powered the Sox back to the top of the standings, and they entered the World Series as heavy favorites against the Cincinnati Reds. Rumors of a fix began swirling even before the first pitch of the series but increased in volume after the underdog Reds took five of eight games for the Championship. During ensuing legal proceedings, Jackson admitted to receiving $5,000 for his participation in the ploy, but his .375 average during the series while charged with no errors in the field, belied his understanding of the payment's purpose. And while the courts found insufficient evidence to convict Jackson and any of his seven co-conspirators of any crime, Commissioner Kenesaw Mountain Landis sentenced all eight to a lifetime banishment from organized baseball.

Thus, at the age of only 32, the 1920 season in which he belted out 218 hits en route to a .382 average marked the final chapter of Jackson's playing career. Perhaps even more stinging, despite collecting

1,772 hits in only nine full seasons and ranking third all-time in career batting average behind only Ty Cobb and Rogers Hornsby, Cooperstown houses no plaque with the inscription of Shoeless Joe Jackson.

Here's the eighth and final game of the infamous 1919 World Series in which the Reds won 10-5. Jackson collected two of the 12 hits he had during the series, including the only home run hit by any of its participants. Included in the line-up were four others who received lifetime bans after the 1920 season: Chick Gandil, Buck Weaver, Happy Felsch, and Swede Risberg. Fred McMullin, the backup third baseman, and pitchers Eddie Cicotte and Left Williams rounded out the group of co-conspirators.

Cincinnati Reds at **Chicago White Sox**
   October 9, 1919

Batting	1	2	3	4	5	6	7	8	9	AB	R	H	RBI
Nemo Leibold CF										5	0	1	0
Eddie Collins 2B										5	1	3	0
Buck Weaver 3B										5	1	2	0
Shoeless Joe Jackson LF										5	2	2	3
Happy Felsch RF										4	0	0	0
Chick Gandil 1B										4	1	1	1
Swede Risberg SS										3	0	0	0
Ray Schalk C										4	0	1	0
Bill James P										2	0	0	0
Roy Wilkinson P										1	0	0	0
Eddie Murphy PH										0	0	0	0
Runs	0	0	1	0	0	0	0	4	0				
Left on Base													

2B: Eddie Collins; Buck Weaver; Shoeless Joe Jackson

3B: Chick Gandil

HR: Shoeless Joe Jackson

HBP: Eddie Murphy

2-Out RBI: Chick Gandil; Shoeless Joe Jackson

Team LOB: 8

Reached on Error: Swede Risberg (produced a run)

Hint: Hod Eller had two strecthes of retiring seven consecutive hitters that were separated by only one at-bat.

Pitching	IP	H	R	ER	BB	BF
Hod Eller	9	10	5	4	1	40

SOLUTION   Shoeless Joe Jackson

Batting	1	2	3	4	5	6	7	8	9	AB	R	H	RBI
Nemo Leibold CF	H	X			X			X	X	5	0	1	0
Eddie Collins 2B	H		X		X			H,R	H	5	1	3	0
Buck Weaver 3B	X		X			H		H,R	X	5	1	2	0
Shoeless Joe Jackson LF	X		H,R,I			X		H,R,2I	X	5	2	2	3
Happy Felsch RF	X		X			X		X		4	0	0	0
Chick Gandil 1B		X		X		X		H,R,I		4	1	1	1
Swede Risberg SS		W		X			X	E		3	0	0	0
Ray Schalk C		H		X			X	X		4	0	1	0
Bill James P		X			X					2	0	0	0
Roy Wilkinson P							X			1	0	0	0
Eddie Murphy PH									HBP	0	0	0	0
Runs	0	0	1	0	0	0	0	4	0				
Left on Base	2	2	0	0	0	1	0	1	2				

The White Sox had a total of 40 plate appearances during the game, meaning every position in the line-up stepped into the batter's box four times, with the top four getting an additional trip to the plate. Those charged with fewer at-bats than plate appearances were Risberg who received the lone walk issued by Eller and Murphy who was hit by a pitch.

9th Inning

The 40th and final batter, Hod Eller faced was Shoeless Joe Jackson, so he was out to end the game and the 1919 World Series.

Murphy had only one plate appearance during the game, here in the 9th, so he had to reach base after being hit by a pitch, as disclosed in the notes.

8th Inning

The White Sox tallied four runs during the 8th, so each of the four batters who scored during the game had to reach base this inning: Collins, Weaver, Jackson, and Gandil. Each reached on a base hit as none of the four walked during the game.

Felsch was out as he failed to reach base during the game.

Gandil had to collect his RBI this inning, as he had no other hits for the game.

Jackson is the only other White Sox hitter credited with any RBIs for the game. Gandil's RBI came with two outs, thus the retirement of Felsch this inning had to account for the second out of the inning. With Felsch behind Jackson in the order, that means any of the runs driven in by Jackson this inning had to come with less than two outs. But one of Jackson's three RBIs did come with two outs, per the notes, so he was limited to driving in only two runs this inning.

The fourth run must have been a result of the error which allowed Risberg to reach base. As the error produced a run, no RBI was credited to Risberg.

Schalk had to make the final out of the inning so that Murphy could lead off the 9th.

Leibold had to account for the first out of the inning so as not to score ahead of Collins.

3rd Inning

Jackson now owns the only unrecorded run scored and RBI. Hence, his home run off Eller had to occur during the 3rd to account for the tally this inning.

As this RBI had to come with two outs, both Collins and Weaver were the first two outs of the inning as Jackson's homer was a solo shot.

Felsch was retired as he had no hits or walks during the game.

1st and 2nd Innings

Leibold could not have reached base during the 3rd inning, as again, no one was on base for Jackson's HR. Thus, Leibold was out to end the 2nd.

James went hitless for the game, so he was the second out of the 2nd.

Jackson, Felsch, and Gandil have no unrecorded hits or walks remaining, so each had to be out during their first at-bat of the game. Only one of these three could have come to the plate during the 2nd inning, as two outs are already recorded. That means at least the first two of these three, Jackson and Felsch had to account for two of the outs in the 1st.

Per the hint, Eller set down seven White Sox in succession on two occasions. If Gandil were the final out of the 1st, that would leave Risberg to lead off the 2nd. For the inning to stretch out to Leibold for the final out, either Risberg or Schalk would have to reach base. If Gandil led off the 2nd with an out, both Risberg and Schalk would have to get on base. Either way, the first two innings of the game will not account for Eller's initial stretch of retiring seven consecutive hitters. The two stretches then had to occur between the end of the 3rd and the start of the 8th.

4th through 7th Innings

Beginning with Felsch's out to end the third, the next six batters appearing in the 4th and 5th innings were retired to account for one of Eller's stretches of seven retired.

Working backward from Leibold's out to lead off the 8th, the six batters preceding him during the 6th and 7th innings were all retired.

That leaves Weaver as the culprit in breaking up the streak with one of his two hits while leading off the 6th.

<u>Back to the 1st and 2nd Innings</u>

With Weaver's two hits now recorded, he had to account for the first out of the game.

That means both Leibold and Collins had to get on base during the 1st via hits.

As Gandil's hit was already recorded, he was retired to start the 2nd.

Risberg drew a walk to complete his line.

Schalk reached on a hit to complete his line.

<u>Back to the 9th Inning</u>

Leibold and Weaver had to account for the other two outs this inning as their hits were already recorded.

Collins reached on the last of his three hits to complete his line.

10. Miguel Cabrera

Jorge Rueda of the Associated Press once wrote that baseball players alongside beauty queens and oil rank as Venezuela's biggest exports. In a testament to such decree, the nation has shipped the likes of Dave Concepcion, Johan Santana, and Andres Galarraga to the MLB. Of the 1,495 players who appeared in the MLB in 2022, 106 hail from Venezuela, including Jose Altuve, Salvador Perez, and Ronald Acuna Jr. The nation of 25 million nestled within a soccer-crazed continent trails only the Dominican Republic for those born outside the US. And though Cooperstown currently houses only one Venezuelan, Luis Aparicio, Miguel Cabrera seems certain to join his fellow countryman upon his retirement.

By the age of 14, Cabrera had already caught the eye of the Tigres de Aragua of the Venezuelan professional winter league. Many of the American baseball teams had also taken note of the young phenom, but MLB rules prohibited the signing of anyone under the age of 16. After waiting out those two years, the Florida Marlins won the sweepstakes for Cabrera's service with a $1.8 million contract. His three-year apprenticeship in the minors plateaued at the Double-A level where he appeared in only 69 games before being called up to the majors. His .365 batting average and .609 slugging percentage while down on the farm, gave manager, Jack McKeon the confidence to immediately insert the 20-year-old Cabrera into his starting line-up. The rookie wasted no time in displaying his offensive prowess, belting an 11th-inning walk-off home run during his June 20, 2002, debut. His promotion helped spark a turnaround for the Marlins who rose from fourth place in the NL East standings before his arrival, to a wild card berth and World Series title.

Since making his debut with the Marlins and moving on to the Tigers in 2008, Cabrera had assembled one of the most prodigious offensive portfolios in the history of the game. At the close of the 2022 season, Cabrera's career numbers read 507 home runs, 3,088 hits, 1,847 RBIs, and a batting average of .308. After collecting hit number 3,000 on April 23, 2022, he joined Hank Aaron and Willie Mays as the only players with 500 or more home runs, 3,000 hits, 1,800 runs driven in, and a .300 average. Cabrera put together his best season in 2012 when he became the first player to win the triple crown since Carl Yastrzemski in 1967 with 44 home runs, 139 RBIs, and a .330 batting average. He nearly repeated the achievement the following year with a league-leading .348 average, but his 44 home runs and 137 RBIs both ranked second. The Baseball Writers Association of America deemed the 2013 performance sufficient, however, to garner Cabrera his second consecutive MVP Award. In 20 seasons through the end of 2022, Cabrera has slashed .308/.384/.524 for an OPS of .908, finished in the top 15 in the MVP ballot on twelve occasions, and appeared in twelve all-star games.

Here's a game from that 2012 season in which Cabrera boosted his triple-crown chances with a 3-for-4 performance, two home runs, and six RBIs. Max Scherzer took the mound to start for Detroit but lasted only two innings due to shoulder fatigue. The bullpen finished the game, allowing only one additional run as the Tigers easily defeated the visiting A's by a score of 12-2. The win put the Tigers at 78–69 for the season and 3 games behind the division-leading White Sox. Within a week, after Chicago lost six of seven, the Tigers pulled even and eventually claimed the AL Central Division with 88 wins, their second of four consecutive division titles. After topping Oakland and New York to advance to the World Series, they were swept by San Francisco in the fall classic.

Oakland Athletics at **Detroit Tigers**

September 18, 2012

Batting	1	2	3	4	5	6	7	8	9	AB	R	H	RBI
Austin Jackson CF										5	3	3	1
Quintin Berry LF										4	0	2	2
Avisail Garcia RF										1	1	1	0
Miguel Cabrera 3B										4	3	3	6
Prince Fielder 1B										3	1	1	2
Delmon Young DH										5	0	0	0
Andy Dirks RF-LF										5	0	0	0
Jhonny Peralta SS										3	1	1	1
Omar Infante 2B										3	1	0	0
Gerald Laird C										3	2	3	0
Runs	1	1	1	0	2	3	0	4	x				
Left on Base													

2B: Miguel Cabrera (off A.J. Griffin); Austin Jackson (off Evan Scribner); Quintin Berry (off Evan Scribner)

HR: Jhonny Peralta (off A.J.Griffin); Miguel Cabrera 2 (off A.J Griffin and off Jesse Chavez);
   Prince Fielder (off A.J Griffin)

SF: Miguel Cabrera (off A.J. Griffin)

HBP: Prince Fielder (by Jesse Chavez)

HIDP: Delmon Young

2-Out RBI: None

Team LOB: 6

Runners retired on the bases: Peralta forced out at 2B

Reached on a FC: Omar Infante

Hint: Omar Infante's walk came two innings prior to Jhonny Peralta's

Pitching	IP	H	R	ER	BB	BF
A.J. Griffin	4.2	8	5	5	1	23
Pedro Figueroa	0.1	0	0	0	0	1
Evan Scribner	1	2	3	3	3	8
Jesse Chavez	1	4	4	4	0	8
Jerry Blevins	1	0	0	0	0	2

Jesse Chavez faced five batters in the 8th inning.

SOLUTION   **Miguel Cabrera**

Batting	1	2	3	4	5	6	7	8	9	AB	R	H	RBI
Austin Jackson CF	H,R	X		X		H,R,I		H,R		5	3	3	1
Quintin Berry LF	H		X		X	H,2I				4	0	2	2
Avisail Garcia RF								H,R		1	1	1	0
Miguel Cabrera 3B	SF,I,X		H,R,I		H,R	X		H,R,4I		4	3	3	6
Prince Fielder 1B	X		X		H,R,2I	W		HBP		3	1	1	2
Delmon Young DH	X		X		X	X		XX		5	0	0	0
Andy Dirks RF-LF		X		X	X		X	X		5	0	0	0
Jhonny Peralta SS		H,R,I		X		W,X	X			3	1	1	1
Omar Infante 2B		X		W		FC,R	X			3	1	0	0
Gerald Laird C		H		H		W,R		H,R		3	2	3	0
Runs	1	1	1	0	2	3	0	4	x				
Left on Base	1	1	0	2	0	2	0	0	x				

Having sent 42 batters to the plate during the game, the first six positions in the Tiger's order had five plate appearances while the bottom three had only four. Those charged with fewer at-bats than plate appearances were Cabrera with an SF, Fielder with an HBP and a walk, and each of the last three who drew a base-on-balls.

8th Inning

Jerry Blevins wrapped up the 8th inning while throwing to only two batters, the 41st and 42nd hitters of the game for the Tigers and recording all three outs. This, of course, had to come with the help of a double play. Per the notes, Young hit into the DP as the 41st batter and he was followed by Dirks for the final out of the inning.

Chavez pitched to the preceding five batters and failed to retire any of them as he recorded no outs beyond his work in the 7th.

Fielder was hit by a pitch from Chavez, per the notes.

Cabrera, Garcia, Jackson, and Laird all reached on hits as Chavez did not give up any walks. Per the notes, Cabrera's safety was a home run off Chavez.

With Cabrera having cleared the bases, Fielder must have been the one retired on the front end of Young's DP, leaving Laird, Jackson, Garcia, and Fielder to account for the four runs scored this inning.

Cabrera had to pick up at least three RBIs, as Jackson was the only hitter in front of him this inning with an RBI. We will come back to determine who drove in that last run.

7th Inning

Having accounted for all four hits allowed by Chavez and five of the eight batters he faced during the game, leaves only three batters remaining and no additional hits allowed. Thus, all three batters Chavez faced in the 7th, Dirks, Peralta, and Infante were retired.

6th Inning

Young was the 32nd batter of the game for the Tigers, and the final hitter to face Scribner, so he was out to end the inning.

Per the notes, both Jackson and Berry doubled off Scribner and, thus, accounted for the two hits he allowed.

Scribner gave up three walks to the remaining five batters he faced this inning. Peralta, Infante, Larid, and Fielder all received a walk at some point during the game. Per the hint, Infante's walk preceded Peralta's, so Infante could not have received a free pass this inning. That leaves the other three to have drawn the walks and Cabrera and Infante to account for the first two outs of the inning

Fielder could not have scored this inning as there was no one left behind him in the order to drive him home. Of the runners on base, only Peralta, Larid and Jackson scored a run during the game. But Peralta's run scored had to occur with his home run. He thus had to be erased on the bases so as not to score this inning. Hence, Infante reached on the FC disclosed in the notes, forcing out Peralta at second base. Infante then came around to score, as well as Larid and Jackson.

Jackson had men on first and second during his at-bat. His double, therefore, had to account for his one RBI of the game.

Berry had runners at second and third, so he must have picked up his two RBIs with his double this inning. Cabrera's SF came off Griffin, so he could not have driven in the other run. With Jackson's RBI now recorded, Cabrera had to pick up all four RBIs during the 8th.

5th Inning

Dirks was the only batter to face Figueroa and he was retired to end the inning.

Young was out as he failed to reach base at any point during the game.

4th Inning

Laird reached base in each of his four plate appearances during the game. He could not have come to the plate during the 5th as he would have scored the first run of the inning, but Laird's two runs were already recorded. Therefore, Laird's at-bat and hit had to occur during the 4th.

Jackson also had to come to the plate during the 4th as Larid could not have ended the inning with a hit. Jackson had to be out to allow three more hitters to bat during the 5th inning and account for the first out of the inning as well as the two runs scored.

Infante walked this inning; as per the hint, it occurred two innings prior to Peralta's.

Peralta had to come to the plate and account for one of the outs as his only hit was a HR and the Tigers failed to score during the 4th. His walk was already accounted for in the 6th.

Dirks was out as he failed to reach base during the game.

Back to the 5th

Of the three remaining batters this inning, two had to score and one had to account for the first out. As Berry failed to score during the game, he was the one retired.

Fielder had to hit his home run this inning as it is the only remaining way in which he reached base this game. As the home run was his only means of producing any RBIs, he had to pick up both this inning.

Cabrera had to collect his double this inning so that he could allow Fielder to drive him in on the home run.

3rd Inning

Young was out to end the inning as he failed to reach base during the game.

Fielder was also out as his three instances of reaching base are all accounted for.

2nd Inning

Peralta's home run off Griffin had to occur this inning. The 3rd extended no further than Young. The 1st inning could not plausibly extend to Peralta, with the Tigers scoring only one run and having no 2-out RBIs.

Infante was out to complete his batting line.

Again, there were no 2-out RBIs during the game, so, at most, there could have been one out when Peralta stepped to the plate. That means Laird had to bat this inning and as he reached base every plate appearance, he collected the first of his three hits.

Jackson's last remaining hit must have been reserved for the inning in which he scored, so he was out.

Back to the 3rd Inning

Cabrera had to hit his home run off Griffin this inning, to account for the one run scored, as there was no one in front of him, this inning, who scored, and there was no one behind him to drive him home.

Berry was retired to account for the first out of the inning so as not to score on Cabrera's home run.

Jackson reached on a hit and eventually came around to score to complete his line.

Berry reached on the first of his two hits to complete his line.

Cabrera picked up the first of his six RBIs with the SF off Griffin to complete his line.

Fielder and Young were both out to complete their batting lines.

Dirks was out to lead off the 2nd to complete his line.

11.   2018 Boston Red Sox

After winning their third World Series Championship during a ten-year span in 2013, the Boston Red Sox slumped to two consecutive 5th place showings in the AL Eastern Division. Disappointed with the production trickling out from one of baseball's highest payrolls, owner, John Henry, hired Dave Dombrowski as President of Baseball Operations in August of 2015 to right the ship.

Dombrowski began his rebuild by shoring up the pitching staff which allowed the second most runs scored in the AL during 2015. He parted with four prospects in return for closer Craig Kimbrell and acquired 2012 Cy Young Award winner, David Price, through free agency during the 2015 off-season. He sent another basket of prospects to the White Sox to obtain Chris's sale after the 2016 campaign. While those moves helped to push Boston back to the top of the Division and into the postseason in 2016 and 2017, the Sox exited the playoffs early in each of those two years, losing in the first round.

With David Ortiz having retired after the 2016 season and the Sox accounting for the fewest home runs in the AL during 2017, Dombrowski turned his attention to the offense. He signed free-agent, J.D. Martinez two weeks into the 2018 spring training session while releasing the underperforming Pablo Sandoval and Hanley Ramirez. He also changed managers, bringing in former Red Sox infielder, Alex Cora. With the table now set, Boston embarked on a historic season.

Martinez joined Mookie Betts and Xander Bogaerts to create an offensive juggernaut, leading the majors in runs scored, hits, doubles, RBIs, batting average, on-base percentage, slugging, and total bases. Combined with the revamped pitching staff that allowed the third-fewest runs in the league, the 2018 Boston Red Sox set a franchise mark with 108 regular season wins. They waltzed through the postseason, losing only three games over the full three rounds, and claimed their 4th World Series title since the turn of the century.

Here's a game from July 12 of the 2018 season in which Boston defeated the Toronto Blue Jays by a score of 6-4. Mookie Betts contributed to his MVP credentials with two hits, including a home run, and five RBIs. Price won his 10th game of the year, going 6.2 innings, allowing six hits and no walks while giving up three runs. Kimbrel closed out the game to earn his 29th save of the season. The win marked their tenth consecutive victory and put the Red Sox at 66-29, 3.5 games ahead of the New York Yankees for the AL East Division lead.

Toronto Blue Jays at **Boston Red Sox**

July 12, 2018

Batting	1	2	3	4	5	6	7	8	9	AB	R	H	RBI
Mookie Betts RF										4	1	2	5
Andrew Benintendi LF										4	0	0	0
J.D. Martinez DH										4	0	1	0
Steve Pearce 1B										0	0	0	0
Blake Swihart 1B										3	0	1	0
Xander Bogaerts SS										4	1	1	0
Brock Holt 2B										4	0	0	0
Eduardo Nunez 3B										4	1	1	0
Sandy Leon C										3	1	0	1
Jackie Bradley CF										2	2	2	0

Runs   0   0   0   5   0   0   1   0   x

Left on Base

2B: Jackie Bradley (off John Axford); Blake Swihart (off Seunghwan Oh)

HR: Mookie Betts (off J.A. Happ)

HBP: Steve Pearce (by J.A. Happ)

HIDP: Andrew Benintendi

Reached on Error: Brock Holt

Reached on FC: Sandy Leon

2-Out RBI: Mookie Betts 4

Team LOB: 4

WP: J.A. Happ (to Jackie Bradley)

Pitching	IP	H	R	ER	BB	BF
J.A. Happ	3.2	5	5	0	1	19
Joe Biagini	2.1	0	0	0	0	7
John Axford	1	2	1	1	0	4
Seunghwan Oh	1	1	0	0	0	4

SOLUTION   2018 Boston Red Sox

Batting	1	2	3	4	5	6	7	8	9	AB	R	H	RBI
Mookie Betts RF	X		X	H,R,4I			H,I			4	1	2	5
Andrew Benintendi LF	X		X	X			XX			4	0	0	0
J.D. Martinez DH	H		X		X		X			4	0	1	0
Steve Pearce 1B	HBP									0	0	0	0
Blake Swihart 1B				X	X			H		3	0	1	0
Xander Bogaerts SS	X			H,R	X			X		4	1	1	0
Brock Holt 2B		X		E,X		X		X		4	0	0	0
Eduardo Nunez 3B		X		H,R		X		X		4	1	1	0
Sandy Leon C		X		FC,R,I		X				3	1	0	1
Jackie Bradley CF			H	W,R			H,R			2	2	2	0
Runs	0	0	0	5	0	0	1	0	x				
Left on Base	2	0	1	0	0	0	0	1	x				

The Red Sox sent 34 batters to the plate during the game, which means every position in the order had four plate appearances except for the last two, who only stepped into the batters' box three times. Those charged with fewer at-bats than plate appearances were Pearce, who was hit by a pitch, and Bradley, who drew the lone walk issued by the Blue Jays.

4th, 5th and 6th Innings

Biagini replaced Happ in the 4th with two outs. During his 2.1 innings, he retired all seven batters he faced. The first was the 20th batter in the lineup, Benintendi, to end the 4th. He then set down each of the three batters in the 5th and 6th.

8th Inning

Oh pitched to the 31st through 34th batters. Of those four, he gave up only one hit, which per the notes, was a double to Swihart. The other three, Bogaerts, Holt, and Nunez, were all out.

4th Inning

The Red Sox scored five runs during the inning, so each of the five players who scored during the game had to reach base this inning: Betts, Bogaerts, Nunez, Leon, and Bradley. (Bradley could have, theoretically, scored both his runs during the inning, but he had only three plate appearances for the entire game, so two of those at-bats could not have come during the same inning)

Bogaerts and Nunez had to reach on their lone hits, as neither drew any walks during the game.

Leon scored this inning, so he had to reach base, but as he had no hits or walks, he had to benefit from the FC disclosed in the notes.

64

We will come back to Bradley to determine whether he reached by a hit or a walk.

Per the notes, Betts homered off Happ at some point in the game. As the 4th inning was the only frame in which Happ allowed any runs, the home run had to occur here.

Before giving up the home run to Betts, Happ recorded two outs in the inning per his pitching line. As neither Swihart nor Holt was credited with any runs scored, they could not have been on base during Betts's home run and were therefore retired this inning. One of these came in relation to Leon's FC. As Swihart's lone hit was already recorded, he never reached base this inning and accounted for the first out. That leaves Holt to have been forced out, but as he had no hits or walks during the game, he must have reached on the error disclosed in the notes.

Betts had to pick up four RBIs this inning as the only other Red Sox credited with a run driven in was Leon and he had only one. With Betts limited to four this inning, Leon had to pick up his on the FC.

7th Inning

Axford came in to pitch the 7th. He recorded three outs while giving up two hits but faced only four batters. Therefore, someone must have been erased after reaching base safely. Per the notes, Benintendi grounded into a double play at some point, so that had to occur this inning.

Martinez was the last batter to face Axford, so he was out to end the inning.

That leaves the other two batters this inning, Bradley and Betts, to collect the hits, the former on a double as disclosed in the notes.

Betts' hit had to push Bradley across the plate to account for the run scored this inning and his 5th RBI.

3rd Inning

Martinez had to end the 3rd. Had he led off the 4th with a hit, he would have scored in front of Bogaerts, but Martinez was not credited with any runs scored. Had he led off with an out, the inning would not have extended past Leon.

Benintendi had no hits or walks for the game, so he was out.

Betts's two hits are already recorded, so he was out.

1st Inning

Betts and Benintendi were both out to complete their lines.

Martinez reached on a hit to complete his line.

As this is Pearce's only plate appearance during the game, his HBP noted in the box score had to occur at this point.

Bogaerts made the final out of the inning to complete his line.

2nd Inning

Holt, Nunez, and Leon were all out to complete their lines.

Jackie Bradley

Bradley reached base during each of his three plate appearances. His first had to come while leading off the 3rd as he could not have ended the 2nd with a walk or a hit.

Bradly also reached on a hit or walk during the 4th. Both these appearances were against Happ. Note in the box score that Happ threw a wild pitch against Bradley. For the pitcher to be charged with a wild pitch, a base runner must advance. While leading off the 3rd, no one would be on base, so the WP had to occur during the 4th. Reconstructing the 4th, that wild pitch would have left runners at 2nd and 3rd with two outs. Had Bradley gotten a hit, it is nearly certain that at least one run would have scored, but since Bradley had no RBIs for the game, he must have walked. The hit, therefore, came in the 3rd.

12.   2016 Chicago Cubs

Chicago Cub fans suffered through the longest stretch of futility ever experienced by a major league sports franchise, enduring more than a century without a championship title. After yet another lost season, the faithful habitually consoled each other with the faintly optimistic assurance of, "wait 'til next year," and pinned the source of their woes on some long-ago scorned billy goat.

The Cubs fixed their hopes of ending the drought on Theo Epstein, who, while in Boston, finally laid rest to the curse of the Bambino. Joining the Cubs before the 2012 season, he began by shedding payroll and rein-vesting in analytics and minor league development. The moves initially put the Cubs in reverse as they sank to a nearly 50-year low in losing 101 games during that first season. But the tank and rebuild strategy slowly began to show dividends with top 10 draft choices such as Kris Bryant, Javier Baez, and Kyle Schwarber. Crafty trades for relatively unknowns, Anthony Rizzo, Kyle Hendricks, and Jake Arrieta along with the free agent signings of David Ross and Jon Lester rounded out the new central cast. With new manager, Joe Maddon at the helm, the small Bears returned to the postseason in 2015 with 97 wins and a wild-card berth. Though they fell to the Mets in the National League Championship Series, hopes for the following season and the end of the spell reached fever pitch.

The pitching staff delivered on those tall expectations, allowing 50 fewer runs than any other club in the majors during the 2016 regular season. The three starters at the top of the rotation, Lester, Arrieta, and Hendricks combined for 53 wins. Hendricks's 2.13 ERA bested all major league hurlers with Lester posting a 2.44 as runner-up. All three finished in the top ten on the NL Cy Young ballot. To bolster the bullpen, Epstein made a move at the trade deadline to acquire the flame-throwing Aroldis Chapman who converted on 16 of his 18 save opportunities.

Prospects for the offense seemed to dim early in the season when Schwarber tore an ACL after only two games and missed the remainder of the season. But Rizzo and Bryant filled out the heart of the order, each slugging over 30 home runs, driving in more than 100 runs, and eclipsing a .900 OPS. Bryant also led the NL with 121 runs scored and picked up the MVP trophy to go along with Rookie of the Year honors from the prior year.

With both sides of the team clicking, the Cubs finished with 103 wins to easily capture the NL Central crown by 17.5 games. After setting down the Giants and Dodgers during the first two rounds of the play-offs, they defeated the Cleveland Indians in seven games, to claim the franchise's first World Series title since 1908.

Here's a game from that 2018 season in which the Cubs visited their division rival, St. Louis Cardinals. Rizzo led the offensive attack with two home runs as the Cubs put up seven runs against four different Cardinal pitchers. Lester blanked St. Louis during his eight innings of work and gave up only three hits and one walk while striking out eight in securing his 17th win of the season. Hector Rendon finished the shut-out to pick up the save.

Chicago Cubs at St. Louis Cardinals
September 14, 2016

Batting	1	2	3	4	5	6	7	8	9	AB	R	H	RBI
Dexter Fowler CF										5	0	2	0
Kris Bryant LF										5	1	1	1
Anthony Rizzo 1B										5	2	2	3
Ben Zobrist 2B										4	0	1	0
Addison Russell SS										4	0	0	0
Jason Heyward RF										3	1	2	0
Javier Baez 3B										4	1	1	0
David Ross C										4	1	1	2
Jon Lester P										3	0	1	1
Jorge Soler PH										1	1	1	0
Runs	0	0	1	0	2	1	0	0	3				
Left on Base													

2B: Javier Baez (off Carlos Martinez)

3B: Kris Bryant (off Michael Wacha)

HR: David Ross (off Carlos Martinez); Anthony Rizzo 2 (off Carlos Martinez and off Michael Wacha)

HBP: Ben Zobrist (by Zach Duke)

HIDP: Kris Bryant

2-Out RBI: Anthony Rizzo 2; Kris Bryant

Team LOB: 6

Pitching	IP	H	R	ER	BB	BF
Carlos Martinez	6	8	4	4	0	26
Jonathan Broxton	1	1	0	0	0	3
Zach Duke	1	0	0	0	1	5
Michael Wacha	1	3	3	3	0	6

SOLUTION   2016 Chicago Cubs

Batting	1	2	3	4	5	6	7	8	9	AB	R	H	RBI
Dexter Fowler CF	X		X		H		H		X	5	0	2	0
Kris Bryant LF	X		X		X		XX		H,R,I	5	1	1	1
Anthony Rizzo 1B	X			X		H,R,I		X	H,R,2I	5	2	2	3
Ben Zobrist 2B		X		X		H		HBP	X	4	0	1	0
Addison Russell SS		X		X		X		X		4	0	0	0
Jason Heyward RF		X			H,R	H		W		3	1	2	0
Javier Baez 3B			H,R		X	X		X		4	1	1	0
David Ross C			X		H,R,2I	X			X	4	1	1	2
Jon Lester P			H,I		X		X			3	0	1	1
Jorge Soler PH									H,R	1	1	1	0
Runs	0	0	1	0	2	1	0	0	3				
Left on Base	0	0	1	0	1	2	0	2	0				

As the Cubs sent a total of 40 batters to the plate, every position in the order had four plate appearances, with the top four getting a fifth. Those charged with fewer at-bats than plate appearances were Zobrist with an HBP and Heyward with a walk.

9th Inning

The 40th and final batter of the game for the Cubs was Ben Zobrist, so he was out.

Per the notes, Rizzo had a home run off Wacha, and as this was Wacha's only inning of work, that must have occurred here in the 9th.

Note also, that Bryant tripled off Wacha, so that too had to occur this inning. As this was Bryant's only hit of the game, it must have produced his lone RBI as well. Bryant would have then scored on Rizzo's HR, giving Rizzo two RBIs for the inning.

Soler pinch hit for Lester in the 9th, and as this was his only plate appearance of the game, he must have collected his hit this inning and then scored on Bryant's triple.

As Wacha only faced six batters, the remaining two hitters this inning, Ross and Fowler must have been out.

8th Inning

Zach Duke who pitched to the preceding five batters, starting with Rizzo, gave up one walk and per the notes, hit Zobrist with a pitch.

Heyward was the only one to draw a walk during the game, so that had to occur this inning, leaving Rizzo, Russell, and Baez to account for the three outs.

7th Inning

Broxton threw to a total of three batters, giving up one hit and recording three outs. That means whoever reached safely was subsequently retired while on the bases. As the notes disclose, no outfield assist or anyone caught stealing, Bryant must have hit into the double-play.

One of the two preceding batters, Fowler or Lester must have reached on the hit, but as Lester's hit must have produced his RBI, he was out this inning and Fowler was the one who collected the hit.

5th Inning

David Ross had only one hit in the game, a home run off Martinez, per the notes. As this was Ross' only hit, it must have produced both his RBIs as well. As the 5th inning was the only frame in which the Cubs scored more than one run, Ross's home run had to occur in this inning.

6th Inning

Two unrecorded RBIs remain: one belonging to Rizzo and the other to Lester. With Lester leading off the 7th, there is no plausible scenario for him to have picked up the RBI in the 6th. That leaves Rizzo, who drove in the run this inning.

Rizzo did homer off Martinez and as Rizzo's other two RBIs are already recorded; the HR must have occurred this inning to account for his remaining RBI.

The inning stretched to Ross, who made the final out of the inning so that Lester could lead off the 7th.

Baez's hit must have been reserved for the inning in which he scored, so he was out.

Russel failed to reach base during the game, so he was out.

That leaves Zobrist and Heyward to have reached on base-hits to extend the inning to Ross.

Bryant could not have batted this inning, as his remaining at-bats all resulted in outs. Thus, if he had batted in the 6th, the inning could not have extended to Ross. Bryant, therefore, made the final out of the 5th.

3rd Inning

The only unrecorded RBI now belongs to Lester, so that must have occurred this inning on his lone hit.

The two unrecorded runs scored belong to Heyward and Baez. Two of Heyward's at-bats were already recorded, and we know he came to the plate during the 5th, leaving only his first at-bat to record. Being the 6th batter in the line-up, that initial plate appearance could not have occurred any later than the 2nd inning, meaning Heyward did not come to the plate during the 3rd. That leaves Baez to account for the run after reaching on his lone hit, a double off Martinez.

Back to the 5th

With Baez having scored in the 3rd, Heyward must have scored his run during the 5th on Ross's home run after collecting the first of his two hits.

Baez and Lester were retired to complete their lines, with Fowler reaching on a hit to extend the inning to Bryant.

The remaining unrecorded at-bats all resulted in outs as all eight hits allowed by Martinez were now recorded.

13. 1995 Atlanta Braves

The Atlanta Braves appeared in a record 14 consecutive postseasons from 1991 to 2005, discounting the 1994 season which ended prematurely with a player's strike. Fueled by arguably one of the greatest rotations ever assembled, the Braves claimed a division title in each of those 14 years, five National League pennants, and one World Series Championship. With the trio of Tom Glavine, John Smoltz, and Greg Maddux on the roster from 1993 to 2002, the Braves posted the lowest ERA in the National League during their entire span together, other than the two years in which they finished second. Collectively they took home seven Cy Young Awards, Maddox winning a record four in succession, the first coming in 1992 while with the Chicago Cubs. Both Maddux and Glavine collected over 300 victories during their careers and the former joined Smoltz in striking out over 3,000. The remarkable credentials eventually earned each a first-ballot entry to Cooperstown.

The pinnacle of their time together on the diamond came in 1995 with the lone World Series title. The Braves took 90 of 144 games during the shortened regular season with the Big Three accounting for 49 of those victories. Maddux led the charges with 19 wins and a major league-low ERA of 1.63.

On the offensive side of the ball, rookie Chipper Jones joined veterans Fred McGriff, Ryan Klesko, and David Justice in the heart of a line-up that produced the second most home runs in the National League that season. Each of the four clouted over 23 round-trippers, McGriff leading the way with 27 to go along with his 93 RBIs.

Here's a game from that 1995 season in which the Braves traveled up to Canada to take on the Expos. While Klesko and Justice sat out against the left-handed Fassero, Mike Kelly and Marquis Grissom filled in admirably with four hits, four runs, and three RBIs between the two. Smoltz went the distance for the Braves, allowing nine hits but giving up only three runs while striking out eight. The victory sparked a seven-game win streak followed quickly by a nine-game streak starting July 1 which propelled the Braves to the top of the NL East where they remained for the balance of the season. After knocking off Colorado and Cincinnati in the first two rounds of the playoffs, they defeated the Cleveland Indians in six games to claim the Braves first World Series title for the city of Atlanta.

Atlanta Braves at Montreal Expos

June 14, 1995

Batting	1	2	3	4	5	6	7	8	9	AB	R	H	RBI
Mike Kelly LF										4	2	2	2
Jeff Blauser SS										4	1	3	2
Marquis Grissom CF										4	2	2	1
Fred McGriff 1B										5	0	0	0
Chipper Jones RF										5	0	1	1
Javy Lopez C										4	0	2	1
Jose Oliva 3B										4	0	0	0
Mark Lemke 2B										4	1	1	0
John Smoltz P										2	1	0	0
Runs	0	0	1	1	2	0	3	0	0				
Left on Base													

2B: Jeff Blauser (off Jeff Shaw); Marquis Grissom (off Jeff Shaw)

3B: Mike Kelly (off Jeff Fassero)

SH: John Smoltz (off Jeff Fassero)

HBP: Jeff Blauser (by Jeff Fassero); Mike Kelly (by Jeff Shaw)

HIDP: Marquis Grissom; Mark Lemke

2-Out RBI: Mike Kelly; Javy Lopez

Team LOB: 8

Reached on Error: Fred McGriff

Hint: Fassero issued his two walks in the same inning.

Pitching	IP	H	R	ER	BB	BF
Jeff Fassero	6	7	4	4	2	27
Jeff Shaw	0	2	3	3	0	3
Gabe White	0	1	0	0	1	3
Luis Aquino	3	1	0	0	0	9

Jeff Shaw faced 3 batters in the 7th inning.
Gabe White faced 3 batters in the 7th inning.

SOLUTION   1995 Atlanta Braves

Batting	1	2	3	4	5	6	7	8	9	AB	R	H	RBI
Mike Kelly LF	X		H,I		H,R,I		HBP,R	X		4	2	2	2
Jeff Blauser SS	HBP		X		H,I		H,R,I	H		4	1	3	2
Marquis Grissom CF	XX			H,R	W		H,R,I	X		4	2	2	1
Fred McGriff 1B		X		X	X		E		X	5	0	0	0
Chipper Jones RF		X		X	X		H,I		X	5	0	1	1
Javy Lopez C		X		H,I		H	W		X	4	0	2	1
Jose Oliva 3B			X	X		X	X			4	0	0	0
Mark Lemke 2B			H,R		X	X	XX			4	1	1	0
John Smoltz P			SH,X		W,R	X		X		2	1	0	0
Runs	0	0	1	1	2	0	3	0	0				
Left on Base	0	0	1	1	2	1	2	1	0				

The Braves sent 42 batters to the plate during the game, meaning the first six in the line-up had five plate appearances while the last three had only four. Those charged with fewer at-bats than plate appearances were Kelly and Blauser, each with an HBP, and Smoltz with an SH. Smoltz also drew a walk as did Grissom and Lopez.

7th Inning

Jeff Shaw entered the game in the 7th to face three batters, and per the notes, hit Mike Kelly with a pitch and then gave up back-to-back doubles to Blauser and Grissom. As Shaw was charged with three runs, each of them scored as well. If runners had been on second and third for Grissom, his double would have driven in two runs, but as he was credited with only one RBI, Blauser must have knocked Kelly home and then scored on Grissom's hit.

Gabe White followed Shaw to the mound and did not fare much better. He, too, faced three batters, and all three reached base, one on a hit, one on a walk, and someone by other means. Lopez had to draw the free pass as he was the only one of the three batters with a walk during the game. Jones had to collect the hit as McGriff went 0-for-5. As this was Jones's only hit of the game and his only means of driving home a run, he also picked up his RBI this inning, bringing Grissom home. McGriff did reach base this inning, as White recorded no outs, so it must have been on the error disclosed in the notes.

Luis Aquino then came in to finish up the 7th. With the bases loaded and the Braves having already scored their three runs for the inning, Aquino must have finished the frame without allowing anyone to reach base. Hence, both Oliva and Lemke were out. Per the notes, Lemke hit into a double play at some point, so we will have to wait to determine if the DP ended the inning, or if it was extended to Smoltz for the final out.

9th Inning

Lopez was the 42nd and final batter of the game for the Braves, so he was out.

Jones's hit has already been recorded, so he was also retired.

McGriff was out, as he went hitless for the game.

6th Inning

Smoltz ended the inning as he was the 27th and final batter to face Fassero.

Lemke scored one run during the game after reaching on his lone hit. Thus, the hit had to come during an inning in which the Braves tallied a run. As they failed to score this inning, Lemke was out.

Oliva failed to reach base during the game, so he accounted for the first out of the inning.

5th Inning

Lopez either ended the fifth or led off the 6th, but either way, McGriff and Jones came to the plate during the 5th and were retired as neither has any hits or walks remaining.

The Braves scored two runs in this inning. Kelly could not have driven in both runs, as only one of his two RBIs came with two outs, so they had to come on separate at-bats. The other run must have been driven in by Blauser. Lopez does have an unrecorded RBI, but he could not end the inning while reaching base safely. So, both Kelly and Blauser reached base on a hit and collected an RBI this inning.

Lemke and/or Smoltz had to reach safely in the 5th to score on Kelly's RBI hit, but we will come back to determine who scored during this inning.

4th Inning

Lopez could not have led off the 5th. If he had reached on a hit that inning, he would have scored ahead of Lemke or Smoltz, but Lopez was credited with no runs. If he was retired, Oliva who was 0-for-4, would have followed with another out, and thus the frame could not have extended past McGriff. Thus, Lopez batted at some point in the 4th inning.

For the 4th inning to get to Lopez and for the Braves to have tallied a run, McGriff and Jones also had to come to the plate this frame, and both were retired as neither has any remaining means of reaching base.

Lopez and Kelly have the only two unrecorded RBIs, so one of them drove in the run this inning. For Kelly to pick up the RBI this inning, one of three scenarios would have had to unfold. The first involves Lemke leading off with a hit and advancing to second on Smoltz's walk. Kelly's single then would have brought Lemke home, leaving runners on first and second with no one out. Both Blauser and Grissom would then have had to hit safely to extend the inning to Lopez. But as that scenario equates to at least one more run scored, this outcome is implausible. Having Lemke advance to second on Smolt's SH instead of the walk is even less plausible, as Jones then accounts for the final out of the inning. The final scenario has Smoltz drawing the walk and then scoring on Kelly's triple. But again, both Blauser and Grissom would have had to reach on hits to extend the inning past Jones, and with Kelly standing on third base, it's highly unlikely that he would not have scored a second run for the Braves this inning. Thus, Lopez reached on one of his two hits and collected the RBI this inning.

Oliva accounted for the final out of the inning as he went hitless for the game.

3rd and 5th Innings

Kelly has the only remaining RBI, so he had to knock in the one run during the 3rd with one of his two hits.

Either Lemke or Smoltz had to score on Kelly's hit, which means only one of the two could have scored during the 5th. That leaves Kelly to have scored one of the two runs posted by the Braves during the 5th. That he was able to come around on Blauser's single, means Kelly must have tripled.

For Kelly's single in the 3rd to drive in the run, Lemke or Smoltz had to be stationed at least at second base during Kelly's at-bat. With Smoltz having no extra-base hits and no stolen bases, wild pitches, or passed balls disclosed in the notes, it had to be Lemke who reached on a hit this inning and advanced to second on either Smoltz's walk or SH before coming around to score.

With Lemke having scored during the 3rd, Smoltz then had to score during the 5th after reaching base on a walk. That means Smoltz put Lemke in scoring position during the 3rd with his SH.

Kelly drove in his run during the 5th with less than two outs, so the 2-out RBI came in the 3rd. Oliva had to account for one of those outs, as he went 0-for-4 during the game.

With Lemke's lone hit recorded in the 3rd, he must have led off the 5th with an out.

Grissom had to reach base during the 5th to extend the inning to Jones for the final out. With Smoltz having reached on his walk this frame, Grissom drew his walk as well per the hint that Fassero issued both in the same inning.

That leaves Lopez to have led off the 6th with a hit to extend the inning to Smoltz.

Back to the 4th

Grissom, being the only batter in front of Lopez with an unaccounted-for run, must have reached base on one of his hits before being driven in by Lopez.

Blauser could not have been on base ahead of Grissom or he would have scored. With the Braves tallying only one run this inning, and the three outs already recorded, Blauser had to account for the final out of the 3rd.

2nd Inning

McGriff, Jones, and Lopez were all retired to complete their lines.

1st Inning

Kelly was out, as his two hits and HBP were already recorded.

Blauser, per the notes, was hit by a pitch from Fassero. As this is his only remaining at-bat to record against Fassero, the HBP must have occurred this inning.

To end the inning and have McGriff lead off the 2nd, Grissom must have hit into the double-play at this point.

8th Inning

Of the four remaining batters to have faced Aquino, only Blauser has a remaining hit. As the 7th could not have extended past Smoltz, that hit had to occur during the 8th.

That leaves Smoltz, Kelly, and Grissom to account for the three outs for the inning.

This means Lemke hit into the double play disclosed in the notes to end the 7th.

14.   Casey Stengel

Most remember Casey Stengel as the colorful manager of the dynastic New York Yankees and later the hapless New York Mets. And rightfully so. As his plaque in Cooperstown notes, he "won 10 pennants and 7 World Series with New York Yankees. Only manager to win 5 consecutive World Series 1949–1955." But before taking on the reins of leadership, Stengel crafted an admirable resume during his playing days.

Starting in 1912, he patrolled the outfield for the Brooklyn Robins and over the course of his 14-year career, also saw time with the Pittsburgh Pirates, Philadelphia Phillies, New York Giants, and Boston Braves. A lifetime .284 hitter, his best year came in 1914 when he averaged .316 and led the National League with a .404 on-base percentage. He also had some pop in his bat, clubbing six or more home runs in four of his first nine seasons, which prior to Babe Ruth ushering in the live-ball era, put Stengel amongst the NL's top ten each of those four years. Perhaps his most notable round-tripper came on April 26, 1913, when he hit the first home run in the newly opened Ebbets Field.

Stengel also enjoyed success as a player in the postseason, appearing in three World Series. On the winning side only once, he nonetheless slashed .392/.469/.607 with two home runs in his 33 World Series plate appearances.

Here's a game towards the end of Stengel's playing days while with the New York Giants. He joined a powerful line-up that included four fellow future Hall-of-Famers: George "High Pockets" Kelly, Frankie Frisch, Dave Bancroft, and Ross Youngs. The potent offense knocked out 14 hits during this contest with the visiting Philadelphia Phillies, which led to an easy 8-3 win for the home team. Aside from contributing two hits to that offensive barrage, Rosy Ryan went the full nine innings on the mound, scattering seven hits amongst two walks to earn his 10th win of the season. Manager, John McGraw, led his team to a total of 93 victories during that season to capture the NL pennant and a World Series title.

Philadelphia Phillies at **New York Giants**

June 28, 1922

Batting	1	2	3	4	5	6	7	8	9	AB	R	H	RBI
Dave Bancroft SS										5	1	2	1
Johnny Rawlings 2B										5	1	3	1
Frankie Frisch 3B										5	0	0	0
Irish Meusel LF										2	1	0	0
Ross Youngs RF										4	0	1	1
High Pockets Kelly 1B										4	2	2	1
Casey Stengel CF										4	2	3	2
Frank Snyder C										3	1	1	1
Rosy Ryan P										3	0	2	1
Runs	0	2	0	0	2	0	0	4	x				
Left on Base													

2B: Dave Bancroft (off Jessie Winters)

HR: Casey Stengel (off Jessie Winters)

SF: Frank Snyder (off John Singleton)

SH: Rosy Ryan (off Jessie Winters)

Produced RBI on a FC: High Pockets Kelly

2-Out RBI: Johnny Rawlings, Rosy Ryan, Dave Bancroft

Team LOB: 7

Runners retired on the bases: Irish Meusel thrown out stealing while Kelly was up to bat, but not part of a double steal

Pitching	IP	H	R	ER	BB	BF
John Singleton	6	9	4	4	2	28
Jesse Winters	2	5	4	4	0	11

SOLUTION   Casey Stengel

Batting	1	2	3	4	5	6	7	8	9	AB	R	H	RBI
Dave Bancroft SS	X	H		X		X		H,R,I		5	1	2	1
Johnny Rawlings 2B	H	X			H,R		X	H,I		5	1	3	1
Frankie Frisch 3B	X		X		X		X	X		5	0	0	0
Irish Meusel LF	X		W,X		W,R		X			2	1	0	0
Ross Youngs RF		X	X		H,I,X			X		4	0	1	1
High Pockets Kelly 1B		H,R		X	FC,I			H,R		4	2	2	1
Casey Stengel CF		H,R		H	X			H,R,2I		4	2	3	2
Frank Snyder C		SF,X,I		X		X		H,R		3	1	1	1
Rosy Ryan P		H,I		H		X		SH,X		3	0	2	1
Runs	0	2	0	0	2	0	0	4	x				
Left on Base	1	2	0	2	1	0	0	1	x				

The Giants sent 39 batters to the plate during the game, meaning they went through the order four full times with the top three getting an additional plate appearance. Those charged with fewer at-bats than plate appearances were Frank Snyder with an SF and Rosy Ryan with an SH. Irish Meusel drew both walks.

7th Inning

Frank Frisch was the 30th batter for the Giants during the game, and the second to face Winters in the 7th inning. As he failed to reach base at any time during the game, he was out.

Next to the plate was Meusel who reached base twice during the game, both times by walks. As Winters did not issue any walks, Meusel was out this inning as well.

8th Inning

Frisch was the 39th and final batter for the Giants during the game, so he accounted for the last out of the inning.

Per the notes, Stengel homered off Winters so that must have occurred in the 8th as that was the only inning in which the Giants scored while Winters was on the mound.

The notes also disclose that Ryan had an SH against Winters and that Bancroft doubled off him. Those events must have unfolded during this frame as well, as the 8th was the only opportunity Ryan and Bancroft had versus Winters.

As Stengel just cleared the bases with his home run, Snyder had to reach base on his lone hit to make Ryan's SH possible. Snyder, now at second base, would have scored easily on Bancroft's double.

Thus far, two of the four runs scored this inning have been recorded. As Youngs did not score during the game, Stengel's HR at most could have driven in two runners: he and Kelly. This means Rawlings had to follow Bancroft with a hit, driving him in and picking up an RBI for himself.

As noted above, Frisch accounted for the final out of the inning, meaning there was no one behind him to drive in Rawlings, leaving Kelly as the only possibility for the unrecorded run scored this inning. Kelly must have reached on one of his two hits and scored on the home run, giving Stengel two RBIs for the inning.

With all five hits allowed by Winters accounted for, Youngs was out to lead off the 8th, and Rawlings was retired leading off the 7th.

5th Inning

Rawlings had to score this inning, as there is no plausible scenario for him to have scored in the 2nd. At most, six batters could have come to the plate in the first without producing a run. Assuming that happened, Stengel could have reached base to lead off the second and eventually come around to score the first run of the inning. Every batter between him and Rawlings, however, would have had to be retired so as not to score the second run of the inning ahead of Rawlings. That equates to three outs before Rawlings even came to the plate. So, Rawlings reached base on one of his three hits in the 5th and eventually scored.

Snyder and Ryan could not have come to the plate during this inning, as we need at least three hitters to account for the three outs in the 6th. That leaves Youngs and Kelly as the only plausible candidates for the two RBIs this inning. Youngs had to pick up his RBI on his lone hit of the game. Per the notes, Kelly's RBI came as a result of an FC.

Frisch was out, as he failed to reach base during the game.

That leaves Meusel to have scored the second run of the inning. He had to reach base on one of his two walks. With Meusel having scored, it had to be Youngs who was retired on Kelly's FC.

Bancroft could not have led off the inning. If he had reached on a hit, he would have scored ahead of Rawlings, but Bancroft's run scored is already recorded. If he had led off with an out, Kelly's FC would have ended the inning without producing the second run. Thus, Rawlings led off the inning, and Stengel ended it with an out to leave a minimum of three batters available for the 6th.

6th Inning

With only three batters coming to the plate during the inning and no double-plays mentioned in the notes, all three were out.

2nd Inning

The two unrecorded runs belong to Kelly and Stengel. Both had to reach on base-hits.

Snyder and Ryan own the two unaccounted-for RBIs. Thus, Snyder drove in Kelly with his SF and Ryan drove in Stengel with one of his two hits.

Note that Ryan's RBI came with two outs, meaning Youngs led off the inning with an out, as his one hit is already recorded.

4th Inning

Bancroft ended the inning so that Rawlings could lead off the 5th.

Ryan reached on his second hit to complete his line.

Snyder accounted for the second out of the inning to complete his line.

Stengel had to reach on the second of his three hits to complete his line.

Kelly had to account for the first out of the inning, as his two hits and FC are already recorded.

Youngs could not have reached base to lead off the 4th as his lone hit was already recorded. As the three outs of the inning are accounted for, Youngs had to end the 3rd.

1st Inning

Meusel was out to end the inning, but we still have the caught-stealing to account for. It could not have occurred in this inning, as per the clue, Kelley was up at the plate when Meusel was thrown out stealing. So Meusel never reached base this inning.

Frisch was out as he went 0-for-5 during the game.

3rd Inning

Frisch was out to complete his line.

Meusel had to reach base on the first of his two walks to complete his line but was then thrown out trying to steal. Per the notes, Meusel was not part of an attempted double steal, so Rawlings could not have been on base at this time. Hence, Rawlings was the final out of the 2nd.

Cleaning up the remaining at-bats, Bancroft had to reach on a base hit during the 2nd to extend the inning to Rawlings. That means Bancroft was retired in the 1st to complete his line while Rawlings reached base on the first of his three hits.

15. Frank Robinson

Frank Robinson began his 21-year major league career as a 20-year-old outfielder for the Cincinnati Reds in 1956. He quickly made his presence known with 38 home runs and a .558 slugging percentage, earning unanimous consent as Rookie-of-the-Year. He continued to build on his freshman campaign and in 1961 carried the Reds to their first World Series appearance in 21 years. His 32 home runs, 124 RBIs, and league-leading 1.015 OPS that season earned the first of his MVP Awards.

Despite averaging 32 home runs and 100 RBIs per season in his first ten years, owner Bill Dewitt, describing Robinson as "an old 30," traded his star way to the Baltimore Orioles after the 1965 season. Dewitt surely regretted his decision almost immediately as Robinson went on to have a season for the ages in 1966. His .316 average, 49 home runs, and 122 RBIs captured the Triple Crown and garnered his second MVP trophy, making him the first, and still only player to win the award in both leagues.

After leading Baltimore to its first World Series title during that 1966 season, and three more appearances in the Fall Classic over the next five seasons, Robinson parted ways and eventually landed in Cleveland where in 1975, he once again made history. As player/manager, he became the first African American to skipper a major league club.

He retired at the end of the 1976 season with a lifetime .294 average and just 57 hits short of 3,000. His 586 home runs put him 4th on the career list at the time and currently ranks 10th. His on-field exploits earned induction into the Hall of Fame in 1982 on his first ballot.

Here's a game from that 1966 Triple Crown season against the visiting Cleveland Indians. In this early contest during Robinson's initial season in Baltimore, he endeared himself to the new fan base with a 541-foot home run off Luis Tiant that left Memorial Stadium. Joined by fellow future Hall-of-Famers, Luis Aparicio and Brooks Robinson, along with the powerful Boog Powell, the Orioles line-up produced 13 hits en route to an 8-3 victory. Wally Bunker started the game for the O's but allowed 3 runs in only 3.2 innings before being pulled in favor of Frank Bertaina who shut out the Indians for the remainder of the game.

Cleveland Indians at **Baltimore Orioles**

May 8, 1966

Batting	1	2	3	4	5	6	7	8	9	AB	R	H	RBI
Luis Aparicio SS										5	1	2	0
Ryss Snyder CF-LF										5	0	1	0
Frank Robinson RF										3	3	3	2
Brooks Robinson 3B										4	1	1	1
Boog Powell 1B										4	2	2	2
Curt Blefary LF										3	1	2	1
Davey Johnson 2B										4	0	1	1
Vic Roznovsky C										3	0	1	1
Wally Bunker P										2	0	0	0
Frank Bertaina P										2	0	0	0
Runs	3	0	2	0	0	0	3	0	x				
Left on Base													

2B: Curt Blefary (off Luis Tiant); Brooks Robinson (off Tom Kelley)
3B: Frank Robinson (off Tom Kelley)
HR: Frank Robinson (off Luis Tiant); Boog Powell (off Tom Kelley)
HIDP: Davey Johnson
2-Out RBI: Vic Roznovsky; Curt Blefary; Davey Johnson
Team LOB: 6
Advanced on an Error: Boog Powell
Runners retired on the bases: Luis Aparicio out stealing (by Bob Allen)

Pitching	IP	H	R	ER	BB	BF
Luis Tiant	2.2	5	5	4	3	16
Lee Strange	0.1	1	0	0	0	2
Tom Kelley	3	5	3	3	0	14
Bob Allen	2	2	0	0	0	6

Tom Kelley faced 3 batters in the 7th inning.

SOLUTION **Frank Robinson**

Batting	1	2	3	4	5	6	7	8	9	AB	R	H	RBI
Luis Aparicio SS	H,R	X		X		X		H,X		5	1	2	0
Ryss Snyder CF-LF	X	X		H		X		X		5	0	1	0
Frank Robinson RF	H,R,2I		W,R	H			H,R			3	3	3	2
Brooks Robinson 3B	X		X	X			H,R,I			4	1	1	1
Boog Powell 1B	H,R		X	X			H,R,2I			4	2	2	2
Curt Blefary LF	H,I		W,R		X		H			3	1	2	1
Davey Johnson 2B	X		H,I		X		XX			4	0	1	1
Vic Roznovsky C		W	H,I		X		X			3	0	1	1
Wally Bunker P		X	X							2	0	0	0
Frank Bertaina P						X		X		2	0	0	0
Runs	3	0	2	0	0	0	3	0	x				
Left on Base	1	1	2	2	0	0	0	0	x				

The Orioles sent a total of 36 hitters to the plate during the game, so they went through the order four full times, with the top two in the line-up getting an extra turn. Those charged with fewer at-bats than plate appearances were Frank Robinson, Blefary, and Roznovsky, who each drew a walk.

7th and 8th Innings

Tom Kelley took the mound for the 4th, 5th, and 6th innings and held the Orioles scoreless during those three frames. That means all three runs charged to Kelley came during the 7th, and as he threw to only three batters that inning, Frank and Brooks Robinson, and Powell, each had to score. Powell, the 32nd and final batter Kelley faced, had to score via the home run disclosed in the notes.

As Kelley allowed no walks for the game, both Robinsons reached ahead of Powell on base hits before coming around to score.

As Powell was credited with only two RBIs, Brooks Robinson must have knocked in Frank to pick up the other RBI.

Bob Allen followed Kelley to the mound after the home run. He faced only six batters, beginning with Blefary in the 7th while recording six outs and allowing two hits. This means the two hitters who reached safely were subsequently retired on the bases.

Per the notes, Aparicio was caught stealing while Allen was on the mound, so he had to initially reach on a hit during the 8th before being erased. Snyder, who was the 38th and final batter of the game, followed with an out. Bertaina accounted for the first out of the 8th as he failed to reach base in his two at-bats.

The only other instance of someone having been retired on the bases disclosed in the notes is the double-play attributed to Johnson, so that had to unfold during the 7th.

With Powell having just cleared the bases with his home run, Blefary had to reach base safely to put the double play in order. As Kelley issued no free passes during the game, Blefary collected one of his two hits.

That leaves Roznovsky to have ended the 7th with an out and complete Allen's pitching line.

1st and 3rd Innings

Lee Strange came in to wrap up the 3rd and threw to two hitters, the 17th and 18th in the order, Roznovsky and Bunker. Strange gave up one hit and retired the other. Roznovsky is the only one of the two who had a hit during the game, so he reached base and Bunker was out to end the inning.

Frank Robinson scored three runs during the game. It is not likely Robinson came to the plate twice in any one frame as the Orioles never scored more than three runs in an inning. Therefore, Frank Robinson had to score in each of the three innings the Orioles tallied a run, including in the 1st and again in the 3rd.

Brooks Robinson's hit is already recorded, so he was out following Frank Robinson in both the 1st and the 3rd.

Snyder, who was not credited with any runs, had to be out in the 1st so as not to score ahead of Frank Robinson.

For the Orioles to score three runs during the 1st, Powell had to reach base safely to keep the inning moving. With both his hits now recorded, Powell was retired in the 3rd.

Snyder had to end the 2nd with an out. If he had been retired to lead off the 3rd, the inning would not have extended to Bunker for the final out. If Snyder had led off the 3rd with a hit, he would have scored ahead of Frank Robinson, but again, Snyder had no runs scored for the game.

Frank Robinson faced Tiant twice during the game. One at-bat resulted in an HR, per the notes. The other was a walk, as Tiant was the only Indian hurler to give away any free passes. Robinson could have produced one RBI, at most, while leading off the 3rd with an HR, leaving a walk in the 1st to produce the other RBI. With Robinson batting third during the 1st, however, a walk cannot produce an RBI. Thus, the HR had to have come during the 1st, and the walk in the 3rd. Obviously, the walk did not create an RBI in the 3rd either, so both Robinson's RBIs came in the 1st. Aparicio had to score on the homer after reaching base on one of his two hits.

2nd Inning

With Aparicio's two hits now recorded, he had to account for the second out of the 2nd inning.

Bunker was out, as he went hitless for the game.

Roznovsky still has a walk from Tiant to record. That walk could not have ended the 1st, so it had to occur during the 2nd.

Back to the 1st and 3rd Innings

Blefary had to come to the plate during the 1st as only two outs are recorded thus far. He had to account for the RBI, driving home Powell for the third and final run of the inning as Johnson could not end the frame with a hit.

Johnson then made the final out of the 1st so that Roznovsky could lead off the 2nd.

That leaves Johnson and Roznovsky to have picked up their RBIs during the 3rd on their lone hits.

As Blefary's two hits were already recorded, he had to reach on his walk during the 3rd to extend the inning and then score on Roznovsky's hit.

6th Inning

Snyder, as noted before, did not score any runs during the game. Thus, if he had led off the 7th, he would have been retired so as not to score ahead of Frank Robinson. But with all three outs recorded, Snyder had to account for the final out of the 6th.

4th Inning

Aparicio was retired to lead off the inning, as his two hits were already recorded.

Snyder and Frank Robinson reached safely on base hits to complete their batting lines.

Brooks Robinson and Powell accounted for the last two outs to complete their batting lines.

5th and 6th Innings

With the five hits allowed by Kelley, all accounted for, the remaining batters were retired, beginning with Blefary in the 5th through Snyder ending the 6th.

16.   We Are Family – 1979 Pittsburgh Pirates

The Pittsburgh Pirates ruled the National League East during the 1970s, winning six division crowns and finishing as runner-up on three other occasions. They won both their World Series appearances during the decade, the first in 1971 and again in 1979 while rallying to their theme song "We Are Family" by Sister Sledge.

The second of those championships came at the conclusion of a 98-win regular season that manager, Chuck Tanner crafted with the deployment of a well-balanced attack. Willie Stargell and Dave Parker led an offensive assault that generated more runs than any other club in the National League. Both finished amongst the league's top ten in slugging and OPS, earning Stargell the MVP Award on the heels of Parker winning the honors during the prior season. From the leadoff spot, Omar Moreno's 193 hits and 77 stolen bases added up to 110 runs scored, second-best in the league. Bill Madlock added to the offensive punch, bringing his .300+ batting average over from the Giants midway through the season.

A pitching staff led by John Candelaria and Bert Blyleven allowed the third-fewest runs on the senior circuit. Six pitchers contributed ten or more victories with two of those hurlers working primarily in relief. That group included the submarine delivering Kent Tekulve coming out of the pen to collect 10 wins and 31 saves.

Here's a game from that 1979 season, in which the Pirates visited their NL East rival, the Philadelphia Phillies. Although the Phillies kept Parker's bat in check with three walks, "Pops" Stargell still led his family to a 13-hit assault in an easy 9-1 win. Veteran Jim Bibby took the mound for the Pirates and allowed the one run on only four hits over 7.1 innings before giving way to Tekulve to secure the final five outs. The win increased the Pirates lead to 2.5 games over Montreal Expos in the NL East, but the race remained tight down to the end. After securing the division title during the final week of the season, the Pirates swept the Cincinnati Reds 3-0 and advanced to the World Series where they defeated the Baltimore Orioles in seven games.

Pittsburgh Pirates at Philadelphia Phillies

August 13, 1979

Batting	1	2	3	4	5	6	7	8	9	AB	R	H	RBI
Omar Moreno CF										5	1	1	1
Tim Foli SS										5	1	2	0
Dave Parker RF										2	3	0	0
Willie Stargell 1B										5	1	3	0
John Milner LF										3	1	1	4
Bill Robinson LF										0	1	0	0
Bill Madlock 3B										5	0	2	3
Ed Ott C										5	1	2	0
Phil Garner 2B										4	0	1	0
Jim Bibby P										4	0	1	1
Kent Tekulve P										1	0	0	0
Runs	2	0	3	0	0	0	0	1	3				
Left on Base													

2B: Phil Garner (off Tug McGraw); Jim Bibby (off Doug Bird); Willie Stargell (off Doug Bird)

3B: Bill Madlock (off Doug Bird)

HR: Omar Moreno (off Larry Christenson); John Milner (off Larry Christenson)

SF: John Milner (off Larry Christenson)

2-Out RBI: Jim Bibby

Team LOB: 9

Hint: In the two at-bats in which Stargell was retired, Madlock followed with another out during that inning.

Pitching	IP	H	R	ER	BB	BF
Larry Christenson	5	7	5	5	2	24
Tug McGraw	2	2	0	0	0	8
Doug Bird	2	4	4	4	3	13

SOLUTION   We Are Family - 1979 Pittsburgh Pirates

Batting	1	2	3	4	5	6	7	8	9	AB	R	H	RBI
Omar Moreno CF	H,R,I	X		X		X		X		5	1	1	1
Tim Foli SS	X		H,R	H			X		X	5	1	2	0
Dave Parker RF	W,R		W,R	X			X		W,R	2	3	0	0
Willie Stargell 1B	H		X		X		H		H,R	5	1	3	0
John Milner LF	SF,X,I		H,R,3I		X		X			3	1	1	4
Bill Robinson LF									W,R	0	1	0	0
Bill Madlock 3B	H		X		X			X	H,3I	5	0	2	3
Ed Ott C	X		H			X		H,R	X	5	1	2	0
Phil Garner 2B		X	X			H		X	W	4	0	1	0
Jim Bibby P		X		X		X		H,I		4	0	1	1
Kent Tekulve P									X	1	0	0	0
Runs	2	0	3	0	0	0	0	1	3				
Left on Base	2	0	1	1	0	1	1	1	2				

The Pirates sent a total of 45 hitters to the plate during the game, so every position in the order batted five times. Those charged with fewer at-bats than plate appearances were Milner with an SF, Parker who drew three walks, Garner with a walk, and either Milner or Robinson in the fifth spot of the order with another walk.

8th Inning

Madlock was the 33rd batter of the game and the first to face Doug Bird in the 8th. The Pirates scored a run this inning, but as Madlock was credited with no runs scored, he was out.

Bibby had to drive the run home this inning with his double off Bird. The only other candidate is Moreno, but his lone RBI had to result from the home run of Christenson. Milner was taken out of the game after the 7th, so he obviously is removed from consideration.

Of the two remaining batters preceding Bibby to the plate this inning, only Ott was credited with a run scored, so he reached on one of his two hits and scored on Bibby's double.

Bibby's RBI came with two outs, per the notes, so Garner had to be out.

The only time Moreno reached base during the game was his home run off Christenson, so he was out to end the inning.

9th Inning

Kent Tekulve was the 45th and final batter of the game for the Pirates, so he was out.

Bird walked three batters during his two innings of work. As none of those occurred in the 8th, all three were issued this inning to the only three hitters who collected a free pass during the game: Parker, Robinson, and Garner.

Both Stargell and Madlock had to collect their extra-base hits off Bird this inning, as they had no other opportunity to face him.

That leaves Foli and Ott to account for the two remaining outs of the inning.

The notes disclosed no one being retired on the bases, so the first three batters to reach this inning: Parker, Stargell, and Robinson had to account for the three runs scored.

Of the eight batters that came to the plate this inning, only Madlock was credited with any RBIs, so he drove in all three runs with his triple.

3rd Inning

Of the five remaining unrecorded RBIs, four belong to Milner. One of those RBIs came via an SF, meaning the other three came off his home run. As the Pirates scored only two runs in the 1st, the homer had to occur during the 3rd.

As Stargell's run scored was already recorded, he was out.

Moreno's run scored came on his home run, so he did not reach base this inning. As Milner had no 2-Out RBIs, Moreno could not have accounted for an out this inning either, so he did not come to the plate this inning.

That leaves Foli and Parker to have reached base and scored on Milner's HR. Foli reached on one of his two hits and Parker walked.

Relying on the hint, Madlock accounted for one of the outs this inning, as Stargell was retired.

1st Inning

Of the two remaining runs scored, one had to come off Moreno's HR and the other via Milner's SF.

Parker had to reach base and score to account for his remaining run. He reached once again by a walk as he had no hits.

As Foil's run scored was already recorded, he had to be out so as not to score ahead of Parker.

For Milner's SF to remain a possibility, Stargell had to reach base on one of his three hits.

6th and 7th Innings

Milner was the final batter faced by McGraw in the 7th, so he was out.

Stargell had to reach safely as Madlock will not bat this inning and thus was unable to fulfill the scenario laid out in the hint.

Garner was the 26th batter of the game and second to face McGraw during the 6th. He had to collect his double during this at-bat as he wouldn't have another chance to face McGraw.

With McGraw's two hits allowed now recorded, everyone else he faced was out, beginning with Ott in the 6th through Milner to end the 7th.

5th Inning

Madlock was the 24th and final batter Christenson faced, so he was out to end the 5th.

Both Milner and Stargell were out to complete their lines.

4th Inning

Parker was out to complete his line, ending the 4th inning.

Foli reached on his second hit to complete his line.

Moreno and Bibby were both retired as their lone hits were already recorded.

Garner could not have led off the 4th as his walk and hit were already recorded. Therefore, he was out to end the 3rd.

2nd Inning

As mentioned earlier, Moreno could not have come to the plate during the 3rd, so he was out to end the 2nd.

Both Bibby and Garner were out to complete their lines.

Back to the 1st

Madlock collected the first of his two hits to complete his line.

Ott could not have ended the 1st with a hit, so he was the final out of the inning.

Back to the 3rd

Ott reached on a hit to complete his line.

17.   2017 Houston Astros

Beginning in 2011, the Houston Astros suffered through a humiliating three-year stretch of losing more than 100 games per season. By 2015, however, a class of high-draft choices and a group of budding stars pushed Houston back into the postseason. Two years later, in 2017, they captured the franchise's first World Series title.

The Astros won 101 regular season games in 2017, largely due to an explosive offense that topped the American League in runs scored, hits, doubles, total bases, batting average, on-base percentage, and slugging. The team OPS of .823 exceeded any other major league club by .35 points and stood .73 points ahead of the league average. Jose Altuve, a diminutive 5'6'' second baseman, headed the attack with an MVP Award-winning season that included a league-leading 204 hits and a .346 batting average. He, along with veteran Marwin Gonzalez, 2011 draft choice George Springer, and 2012 first-overall draft pick, Carlos Correa, slugged over .522 and belted out at least 23 home runs.

Surprisingly, especially for a team that exceeded 100 wins, Charlie Morton and 2015 Cy Young Award winner, Dallas Keuchel topped the pitching staff with only 14 victories apiece. The late-season addition of Jason Verlander, however, added some needed punch to the rotation as he won all five games he started down the stretch while allowing a total of only four runs.

After taking the American League West Division by 21 games, the Astros defeated the Boston Red Sox three games to one in the ALDS and then downed the New York Yankees in seven games during the ALCS. Having represented the NL in the 2005 Fall Classic, they made history by becoming the first franchise to appear in the World Series as a member of both leagues. But alas, history will remember the Astros most for the scandal that tarnished the 2017 championship. In 2020, an MLB investigation concluded that the Astros had employed a sign-stealing scheme throughout the 2017 campaign, involving the use of video replay cameras to steal opponents' pitching signs and then relaying them to the batter by banging on a trash can. Though commissioner Rob Manfred decided not to vacate the 2017 championship, fans and fellow players have proved less forgiving.

Here's a game from early June of that 2017 season in which the Astros traveled to meet their cross-state rival, the Texas Rangers. Though the Ranger's staff tamed the bats of Altuve and Alex Bregman, Springer, Correa, and 33-year-old rookie Yuli Gurriel led a nine-hit attack that produced a 7-2 win for the visitors. Brad Peacock started the first six innings for the Astros, giving up the two runs on four hits while striking out nine. Three relievers came in to lock up the victory, shutting out the Rangers on only two more hits.

Houston Astros at Texas Rangers
June 4, 2017

Batting	1	2	3	4	5	6	7	8	9	AB	R	H	RBI
George Springer RF										5	2	3	3
Jose Altuve 2B										4	0	0	0
Carlos Correa SS										3	1	2	1
Evan Gattis C										5	1	0	0
Carlos Beltran DH										4	1	1	1
Marwin Gonzalez LF										4	0	1	0
Yuli Gurriel 1B										3	2	2	2
Alex Bregman 3B										3	0	0	0
Jake Marisnick CF										4	0	0	0
Runs	2	1	2	1	1	0	0	0	0				
Left on Base													

2B: Carlos Beltran (off Martin Perez); Marwin Gonzalez (off Martin Perez)

HR: George Springer 2 (2 off Martin Perez); Carlos Correa (off Martin Perez);
   Yuli Gurriel (off Tony Barnette)

SF: Yuli Gurriel (off Martin Perez)

HIDP: Jake Marisnick

2-Out RBI: George Springer; Yuli Gurriel; Carlos Beltran

Team LOB: 7

Reached on Error: Evan Gattis

Pitching	IP	H	R	ER	BB	BF
Martin Perez	3.2	7	6	5	3	21
Tony Barnette	2	1	1	1	2	9
Nick Martinez	3.1	1	0	0	0	11

Batting	1	2	3	4	5	6	7	8	9	AB	R	H	RBI
George Springer RF	H,R,I	H,I		H,R,I		X		X		5	2	3	3
Jose Altuve 2B	X	X		X		W			X	4	0	0	0
Carlos Correa SS	X		H,R,I	W		W			H	3	1	2	1
Evan Gattis C	E,R		X	X		X			X	5	1	0	0
Carlos Beltran DH	H,I		W,R		X		X		X	4	1	1	1
Marwin Gonzalez LF	X		H		X		X			4	0	1	0
Yuli Gurriel 1B		H,R	SF,X,I		H,R,I		X			3	2	2	2
Alex Bregman 3B		W	X		X			X		3	0	0	0
Jake Marisnick CF		XX		X		X		X		4	0	0	0
Runs	2	1	2	1	1	0	0	0	0				
Left on Base	1	1	1	1	0	2	0	0	1				

The Astros sent a total of 41 batters to the plate during the game, so every position in the order had at least four plate appearances with the first five getting an additional chance. Those charged with fewer at-bats than plate appearances, included Gurriel with an SF, Correa with two walks, and Altuve, Beltran, and Bregman each with one walk.

5th Inning

Tony Barnette came in to record the last out of the 4th and pitched through the first two outs of the 6th. During that time, he gave up an HR to Gurriel. As Perez allowed the first six runs of the game, Barnette's lone earned run accounted for the Astro's seventh tally of the game scored here during the 5th off the home run by Gurriel.

Gurriel was credited with two RBIs for the game, one via an SF and the other as a result of the home run. As the SF could not have occurred with two outs, his 2-Out RBI had to come with the home run here in the 5th. Obviously, no one was on base for Gurriel's solo shot, so Beltran and Gonzalez had to account for the two outs before the home run.

The first batter to face Barnette was the 22nd batter of the game or Gattis. Barnette recorded one out during the 4th, and as Gattis was the only batter he faced during that inning, he had to be out.

1st Inning

Correa had only one RBI during the game and thus his HR had to be a solo shot. As he had no 2-Out RBIs for the game, that HR could not have occurred during the 1st.

For Gurriel to drive in a run this inning on the SF, of the six batters ahead of him, five would have had to reach base while scoring only one run. As that is not plausible, only Springer and Beltran are left as viable candidates for the RBIs this inning. Springer had to do so with the benefit of the first of his two home runs. Beltran had to collect his with the double off Perez.

Of the three batters immediately ahead of Beltran, only Correa and Gattis were credited with a run. Correa's, however, came with his home run, leaving Gattis as the one who scored the second run of the inning. As he had no hits or walks for the game, Gattis had to reach on the error disclosed in the notes, thus accounting for Perez's unearned run.

Altuve and Correa had to account for the first two outs of the inning so as not to score ahead of Gattis.

3rd Inning

As determined above, Correa's HR did not come in the 1st. It could not have happened during the 4th either as the following batter, Gattis, ended the inning, meaning, had Correa homered, it would have come with two outs, but Correa had no 2-Out RBIs.

With a runner on base in the first and two outs already recorded, the inning could not extend beyond Bregman without tallying another run. Thus, it is not plausible that Correa came to the plate during the 2nd with fewer than two outs, no one on base, and no runs scored. That leaves the 3rd inning as the only plausible alternative for Correa's solo HR off Perez.

2nd Inning

We are not yet sure if Gurriel came to the plate during the 2nd, but if he did, he would not have been in a position to drive in the run via the SF. That leaves Springer to have collected the RBI this inning on the second of his two base hits.

That also means Altuve made the final out of the inning so that Correa could lead off the 3rd.

Back to the 3rd

Gattis followed Correa's HR with an out, as his only time in reaching base was already recorded.

The remaining unrecorded RBIs belonged to Gurriel and Springer. As the inning could not have extended to Springer before the second run was scored, Gurriel had to drive in the run with his SF.

Beltran was the only hitter between Gattis and Gurriel with a run scored. As Beltran's hit was already recorded, he reached on his walk and scored on Gurriel's SF.

Gonzalez had to reach safely on his lone hit so that there were less than two outs during Gurriel's at-bat.

Back to the 1st and 2nd Innings

With Gonzalez' lone hit now recorded, he was out to end the 1st.

Of the three batters who preceded Springer to the plate during the 2nd, at least one had to reach base to extend the inning back to the top of the order. That means Springer's home run could not have occurred this inning though, as only one run scored. So, of the first three that came to the plate during the 2nd, the one who reached base also had to come around to score on Springer's hit. As Gurriel is the only one of the three credited with a run scored, he reached on the first of his two hits before being driven in by Springer.

Note that Perez faced 21 batters during the game: 11 outs (3.2 innings x 3), plus 7 hits, plus 3 walks. However, Gattis reached on an error while Perez was on the mound, so someone must have been erased on the base paths to keep Perez from facing 22 batters. Per the notes, Marisnick hit into a double play which had to come while Perez was in the game.

Marisnick faced Perez in either the 3rd or 4th, but either way, it could not have resulted in a DP. There were already two outs in the 3rd when Marisnick came to the plate. He might lead off the 4th, but with no one on before him, the DP was not possible.

The only other appearance Marisnick had versus Perez, occurred in the 2nd, so that had to be the inning in which he hit into the DP.

Bregman had to reach on a walk during the inning to extend it to Marisnick. It also had to be Bregman retired on the DP, as Gurriel eventually came around to score.

Back to the 3rd Inning

Bregman had to end the inning with an out, as his walk is now recorded. He was also out to end the 5th.

6th Inning

Marisnick led off with an out, as he went hitless for the game.

Springer was out as his only remaining hit was another HR off Perez.

That leaves Altuve and Correa to collect the two walks Barnette issued before giving way to Nick Martinez to finish the game.

Gattis ended the inning with an out, as he failed to reach base during the game other than the error which was already recorded.

7th, 8th, and 9th Innings

In his 3.1 innings of work, Martinez gave up one hit and no walks. The only two unrecorded hits belong to Springer and Correa. Springer's remaining hit was his second home run against Perez, leaving Correa as the one to gain the hit off Martinez. Everyone else was out, starting with Beltran in the 7th. Completing the innings, Correa faced Martinez only once, during the 9th when the hit occurred.

4th Inning

Completing each player's line, Marisnick led off with an out, Springer hit his second home run, Altuve was out, and Correa walked.

18. Joe Charboneau

Joe Charboneau seemed to come out of nowhere to capture the hearts and imagination of an adoring Cleveland fan base in 1980. While showing some promise in 1976 during his initial season of single-A ball, the 22-year-old slumped to a .172 batting average the following year and walked away from baseball, going home to California to work as a stock clerk in an electronics company. After some convincing, he returned to the minors and promptly hit his way to successive batting titles in 1978 and 1979, averaging .350 and slugging .570 over the two seasons. Invited to Cleveland's spring training camp in 1980 with assumptions of promotion to triple-A, a season-ending knee injury to first baseman, Andre Thornton opened a roster spot for Charboneau. The legend began almost immediately with an opening-day home run during his second major league at-bat. He went on to slug a total of 23 home runs during the season while driving in 87 runs and posting a .289 batting average. Only three years after "quitting" baseball, the Baseball Writers Association of America crowned him the AL Rookie of the Year.

His meteoric rise from a hardscrabble background and his playful personality endeared him to the Cleveland faithful. He drew comparisons to the fictional Joe Hardy from the "Damn Yankees" and the Indians beat writer, Terry Pluto, dubbed him "Super Joe." A local band even composed "Go Joe Charboneau" which climbed to number 4 on the singles chart in Cleveland.

Unfortunately, the descent came just as rapidly. Hampered by a back injury suffered before the 1981 season, Charboneau played in a total of only 70 games over the next two seasons. He hit only six home runs and drove in a total of 27 runs while batting .211 in that limited playing time. He took his last major league at-bat on June 1, 1982, his 201st career game, which stands as a record for the fewest games played in the majors by a position player who won a Rookie of the Year Award.

Here's a game from that electrifying rookie year when Charboneau and his teammates visited the Baltimore Orioles. Super Joe led the Indians' offensive attack that put up seven runs against a typically stingy Baltimore pitching staff. Dan Spillner, Bob Owchinko, and Victor Cruz all threw for the Indians, giving up a total of six runs. The 7-6 win put the Indians at 18-22 for the season and in 6th place in the seven-team AL Eastern Division. Despite the spark provided by Charboneau, the Indians closed out the season in that same spot with a 79-81 record, 23 games out of the lead.

Cleveland Indians at Baltimore Orioles

May 27, 1980

Batting	1	2	3	4	5	6	7	8	9	AB	R	H	RBI
Miguel Dilone LF										4	1	2	0
Rick Manning CF										3	1	1	0
Mike Hargrove 1B										4	1	1	3
Jorge Orta RF										3	0	0	0
Ron Hassey C										4	0	0	0
Toby Harrah 3B										3	2	1	1
Joe Charboneau DH										4	2	2	2
Dave Rossello 2B										3	0	0	0
Cliff Johnson PH										1	0	0	0
Tom Veryzer SS										4	0	2	1

Runs   0   2   0   0   0   3   0   0   2

Left on Base

2B: Rick Manning (off Steve Stone); Joe Charboneau (off Dave Ford)

HR: Joe Charboneau (off Steve Stone); Mike Hargrove (off Steve Stone); Toby Harrah (off Dave Ford)

SH: Rick Manning (off Dave Ford)

HIDP: Toby Harrah

2-Out RBI: Joe Charboneau 2; Tom Veryzer

Team LOB: 2

Reached on Error: Miguel Dilone

Runners Retired on Bases: Veryzer caught stealing third;

   Veryzer thrown out at second attempting to stretch a single into a double;

   Orta erased on the front end of a double-play

Pitching	IP	H	R	ER	BB	BF
Steve Stone	5	5	5	4	2	22
Dave Ford	3.1	3	2	2	0	12
Tim Stoddard	0.2	1	0	0	0	2

Steve Stone faced 4 batters in the 6th inning.

SOLUTION   Joe Charboneau

Batting	1	2	3	4	5	6	7	8	9	AB	R	H	RBI
Miguel Dilone LF	X		H			E,R		H		4	1	2	0
Rick Manning CF	X		X			H,R		SH,X		3	1	1	0
Mike Hargrove 1B	X		X			H,R,3I		X		4	1	1	3
Jorge Orta RF		X		X		W		X		3	0	0	0
Ron Hassey C		X		X		X			X	4	0	0	0
Toby Harrah 3B		W,R		X		XX			H,R,I	3	2	1	1
Joe Charboneau DH		H,R,2I			X		X		H,R	4	2	2	2
Dave Rossello 2B		X			X		X			3	0	0	0
Cliff Johnson PH									X	1	0	0	0
Tom Veryzer SS			H,X		X		X		H,I,X	4	0	2	1
Runs	0	2	0	0	0	3	0	0	2				
Left on Base	0	0	1	0	0	0	0	1	0				

Having sent a total of 36 batters to the plate during the game, every position in the order had four plate appearances. Those charged with less than four at-bats were Manning with an SH, and Orta and Harrah drawing the two walks issued by the Orioles.

9th Inning

Tim Stoddard pitched to the final two batters of the game, the 35th and 36th in the Indians' order: Johnson and Veryzer. He gave up one hit and retired the other.

Johnson had to account for the out as he failed to reach base in his one at-bat.

That leaves Veryzer to have reached on the base hit but note that he was retired on the bases after each of his two hits. As he had no extra-base hits, and no one bats behind him this inning, it is doubtful he was out trying to steal third base this inning. Thus, he must have reached base on a hit but was then thrown out trying to stretch it into a double.

Harrah's HR off Ford had to occur this inning as it was the only inning in which Ford allowed any runs. The three runs scored during the 6th were all charged to Stone. Harrah collected only one RBI during the game, however, so the HR had to be a solo shot.

6th Inning

Stone threw to four batters during the 6th and failed to retire any of them. From the 19th through 22nd batters in the line-up, all four reached base and accounted for the three runs charged to Stone.

The 22nd batter, Orta had to reach on a walk as he had no hits for the game.

106

Per the notes, Hargrove homered off Stone, and as this was his only hit for the game, the HR had to occur this inning. It also accounted for all three of Hargrove's RBIs as no one in front of him this inning, drove in any runs during the game.

Dilone reached on either an error or a hit, but was on board and scored on Hargrove's HR.

Manning had to reach on his lone hit, also scoring on Hargrove's HR.

Hassey was out as he had no hits or walks for the game.

Per the notes, Orta was retired on the front end of a double play at some point during the game. As the 6th was the only time he reached base, the DP had to occur this inning. As disclosed in the notes, Harrah was the one who hit into the twin killing.

Back to the 9th Inning

With no one in front of Harrah having any unrecorded runs scored, Charboneau had to account for the second run of the inning. He must have doubled off Ford, as disclosed in the notes, and then came around to score on Veryzer's hit.

Hassey failed to reach base during the game, so he was retired to account for the first out of the inning.

2nd Inning

As this is the only remaining inning in which the Indians score any runs, Charboneau's HR off Stone had to occur this frame and account for his two RBIs.

The only unrecorded run scored at this point belongs to Harrah, so he had to reach on his walk and score on the HR.

Charboneau's two RBIs came with two outs, so both Orta and Hassey were out.

Rossello was out to end the inning as he failed to reach base during the game.

Quickly going back to the 6th, per Stone's pitching line, he gave up an unearned run. Both runs scored in the 2nd were earned, so the unearned had to occur during the 6th. Dilone reached on an error at some point during the game and it must have come during the 6th so that the run he scored was, in fact, unearned.

1st Inning

All three batters were retired so that Orta could lead off the 2nd.

7th and 8th Innings

Charboneau and Rossello were both retired to start the 7th as neither has any unrecorded hits or walks remaining.

Manning has an SH off Ford remaining. It could not have occurred during the 7th as two outs are already recorded. Hence, the SH had to come during the 8th.

Manning could not have led off the inning with an SH, so Dilone had to reach base on one of his two hits to lead off the 8th, leaving Veryzer to account for the final out of the 7th.

Hargrove and Orta accounted for the final two outs of the 8th so that Hassey could lead off the 9th.

3rd Inning

Dilone had to reach base on a hit to complete his line.

Veryzer has two more at-bats to record, one resulting in a hit. Per the notes, he was subsequently thrown out attempting to steal third base. He does have a remaining at-bat that ends the 5th. But with no one batting behind him that inning to move him over, with no wild pitches or passed ball noted, and Veryzer not being credited with perhaps stealing second base, it is not plausible that he was caught stealing third base that inning. Therefore, Veryzer reached during the 3rd, moved to second on Dilone's single, and was then thrown out trying to steal third.

Manning and Hargrove were out to complete their lines and end the inning.

4th and 5th Innings

As all the hits and walks allowed by Stone are now recorded, the remaining six batters he faced were retired in order starting with Orta leading off the 4th and Veryzer ending the 5th.

19. 1993 Toronto Blue Jays

In 1992, the Toronto Blue Jays became the first franchise outside of the U.S. to win a World Series title. They followed that up with another championship in 1993, with arguably the most thrilling conclusion to a World Series since Bill Mazeroski's heroics in 1960. With the Philadelphia Phillies leading 6-5 going into the bottom of the 9th and hoping to extend the series to a seventh game, they called on their fiery left-handed reliever, Mitch Williams, to preserve the lead. After allowing two of the first three Jays to reach base, Williams faced clean-up hitter, Joe Carter, who crushed a long drive over the left field wall to capture Toronto's second consecutive title.

Most of the names on the roster during those two championship years remained the same with some notable exceptions. After slugging 26 home runs and driving in 108 runs, Dave Winfield departed via free agency after the '92 season but the Jays replaced his bat with their signing of Paul Molitor. They also plucked two aging stars away from the Oakland A's for the '93 team, signing Dave Stewart to a free-agent contract and trading for Rickey Henderson midway through the season.

Molitor fit in nicely with John Olerud and Roberto Alomar to form the nucleus of a stacked offense. Each of the trio reached base above a .400 clip and posted an OPS above .900. Alomar carried the lowest average of the group at .326 and ended up only eight hits shy of all three collecting more than 200 hits. Each finished amongst the top six in the race for AL MVP honors. Joe Carter added muscle to the line-up, leading the team in both home runs (33) and RBIs (121) while finishing 12th on the MVP ballot.

Pat Hentgen led the pitching staff with 19 wins, but three others joined him in collecting double-digit wins: Juan Guzman (14), Dave Stewart (12), and Todd Stottlemyre (11). Duane Ward came out of the pen to save a league-leading 45 games while striking out 97 in only 71.2 innings pitched.

Manager Cito Gaston led his charges to a 95-67 record during the '93 regular season, one less victory than the prior campaign. Topping the AL Eastern Division by seven games, they began the postseason by defeating the Chicago White Sox four games to two in the AL Championship Series before advancing on to the World Series.

Here's game six of that Fall Classic in which Joe Carter ended in dramatic fashion to secure an 8-6 victory for the Jays. Dave Steward started for Toronto and took a 5-1 lead into the 7th inning before giving up a three-run homer to Lenny Dykstra. Danny Cox came in to try to finish the inning but gave up another two runs which put the Phillies ahead 6-5 where the score remained heading into the final frame.

Philadelphia Phillies at **Toronto Blue Jays**

October 23, 1993

Batting	1	2	3	4	5	6	7	8	9	AB	R	H	RBI
Rickey Henderson LF										4	1	0	0
Devon White CF										4	1	0	0
Paul Molitor DH										5	3	3	2
Joe Carter RF										4	1	1	4
John Olerud 1B										3	1	1	0
Roberto Alomar 2B										4	1	3	1
Tony Fernandez SS										3	0	0	0
Ed Sprague 3B										2	0	0	1
Pat Borders C										4	0	2	0
Runs	3	0	0	1	1	0	0	0	3				
Left on Base													

2B: John Olerud (off Terry Mulholland); Roberto Alomar (off Terry Mulholland)

3B: Paul Molitor (off Terry Mulholland)

HR: Paul Molitor (off Terry Mulholland); Joe Carter (off Mitch Williams)

SF: Joe Carter (off Terry Mulholland); Ed Sprague (off Terry Mulholland)

HBP: Tony Fernandez (by Larry Andersen)

2-Out RBI: Roberto Alomar

Team LOB: 7

Hint: Devon White's walk came in the same inning as Molitor's triple.

Pitching	IP	H	R	ER	BB	BF
Terry Mulholland	5	7	5	5	1	23
Roger Mason	2.1	1	0	0	0	8
David West	0	0	0	0	1	1
Larry Andersen	0.2	0	0	0	1	4
Mitch Williams	0.1	2	3	3	1	4

SOLUTION   1993 Toronto Blue Jays

Batting	1	2	3	4	5	6	7	8	9	AB	R	H	RBI
Rickey Henderson LF	X	X		X			X		W,R	4	1	0	0
Devon White CF	W,R	X			X		X		X	4	1	0	0
Paul Molitor DH	H,R,I		X		H,R,I		X		H,R	5	3	3	2
Joe Carter RF	SF,I,X		X		X			X	H,R,3I	4	1	1	4
John Olerud 1B	H,R		X		X			W		3	1	1	0
Roberto Alomar 2B	H,I			H,R		H		X		4	1	3	1
Tony Fernandez SS	X			X		X		HBP		3	0	0	0
Ed Sprague 3B		X		SF,I,X		X		W		2	0	0	1
Pat Borders C		H		H		X		X		4	0	2	0
Runs	3	0	0	1	1	0	0	0	3				
Left on Base	1	1	0	1	0	1	0	3	0				

Forty Blue Jay batters came to the plate during the game, so every position in the line-up had at least four plate appearances with the top four getting a fifth try. Those charged with fewer at-bats than plate appearances were Carter and Sprague each with an SF, Fernandez with an HBP, and Henderson, White, Olerud, and Sprague drawing the walks.

9th Inning

Jumping immediately to the climax of the game, Joe Carter was the 40th and final batter of the evening and as this was his only opportunity versus Mitch Williams, ended the game and series in dramatic fashion with the home run disclosed in the notes. Carter produced one of his four RBIs of the game via the SF, but as he had no other hits, he had to drive in the remaining three runs with HR.

Williams allowed one other hit during his appearance, and as Molitor is the only one of the three batters preceding Carter credited with a hit, he had to reach safely and score on the HR.

Between Henderson and White, one was out and the other reached on the walk allowed by Williams and scored on the HR. Per the hint, White's walk came in the same inning as Molitor's triple. As Molitor's triple came against Mulholland, Henderson reached on the free pass and White was out.

8th Inning

Borders was the last batter to face Andersen during the 8th, so he was out.

Per the notes, Fernandez was hit by a pitch from Andersen. As Andersen faced Fernandez only once, the HBP had to occur in this inning.

Andersen also gave up a walk, but of the two remaining hitters he faced, only Sprague received a walk during the game, leaving Alomar to account for the other out Andersen recorded.

David West threw to only one batter, Olerud, and walked him.

Carter was out as his one hit is already recorded and he received no walks during the game.

7th Inning

Molitor had to end the inning with an out. If he had led off the 8th with an out, the inning could not have extended to Borders. If he had led off the inning with a hit, he would have had to score, as there were two walks and an HBP behind him, but the Jays failed to score this inning.

White was out as the only time he reached base was on a walk, but Mason walked no one.

Henderson was out as he failed to reach base on a hit during the game.

6th Inning

Both Sprague and Fernandez had to come to the plate during the inning and both were out as neither reached on a hit during the game.

Alomar had to reach base on a hit during each of his remaining at-bats to account for his three hits. He could not have ended the 5th with a hit, so he reached here in the 6th.

With Mason's one hit allowed now recorded, Borders had to be out to end the 6th.

1st Inning

Henderson was out as he had no hits for the game and his walk is already recorded.

White had to reach base this inning on his walk. The only 2-Out RBI of the game belonged to Alomar. At least two of the runs driven in this inning had to occur with less than two outs, so the inning could not have begun with the first two batters retired. White will also have to come around to score, as the notes do not disclose anyone having been retired on the bases.

Per the hint, Molitor's triple followed White's walk which would have brought White home.

Carter had to be out this inning as his lone hit was already recorded. He may have knocked in a run with the SF, but we are not able to determine that quite yet.

Olerud had to reach base to keep the inning going so that the Jays could score three runs. His only hit was the double off Mulholland disclosed in the notes so that had to come this inning. The double surely would have driven Molitor home from third base, but Olerud was credited with no RBIs for the game. That means Molitor scored prior to Olerud's at-bat, leaving Carter to have collected the RBI this inning on the SF.

Alomar, as noted before, had to reach base on each of his remaining at-bats. With two outs already recorded and Alomar the only Blue Jay with a 2-Out RBI, the base hit had to drive in Olerud for the third run of the inning.

Fernandez was out as his HBP is already recorded.

5th Inning

Olerud was the 23rd and final batter Mulholland faced to end the 5th, so he was out.

Carter was out as his lone hit was already recorded.

The only two remaining runs scored belong to Molitor and Alomar. Alomar could not have come to the plate this inning and had the frame extend all the way to Olerud, so Molitor reached base on one of his three hits and scored the lone run this inning. As no one behind him could have driven him home, Molitor hit his HR off Mulholland this inning.

Neither Henderson nor White reached base during their remaining at-bats, so White was out to lead off the 5th and Henderson was out to end the 4th.

4th Inning

Alomar had to reach base on one of his three hits and score this inning as he owns the last remaining run scored.

Fernandez was out to complete his line.

Sprague owns the last remaining RBI, so he had to collect it this inning on his SF.

Borders had to reach on one of his two hits to extend the inning to Henderson.

2nd and 3rd Innings

The only hit left to record belongs to Borders which had to come in the 2nd inning.

The remaining batters during the two innings were retired to complete their lines, beginning with Sprague leading off the 2nd and ending with Olerud in the 3rd.

20. Pete Gray

Pete Gray, born Peter J. Wyshner Jr., lost his dominant right arm to amputation as the result of an early child-hood accident. What might seem a devastating loss for anyone dreaming of becoming a major league ball player, hardly deterred the young lad from Nanticoke, PA. The determined Gray taught himself to bat and throw with the use of only his left arm and by the age of 19 began patrolling the outfields of assorted local semi-pro teams. Though proving he could compete with his disability, the pro scouts scoffed at the idea of a one-armed ball player. Not until the age of 25 did he finally receive the opportunity to showcase his talents outside of Pennsylvania. In his two seasons with the Brooklyn Bushwicks, he hit .350 and then moved on to Quebec where he improved to .381 while competing in the Canadian American League. And after hitting .333 with five home runs and 68 stolen bases while earning Southern Association MVP honors in 1944 with the Memphis Chickasaws, the big leagues could no longer ignore the "One-Armed Wonder." The St. Louis Browns purchased his contract, and the 30-year-old rookie made his major league debut the following season.

Despite his success coming up through the minors, skeptics abound, seeing him only as a gate attraction for the ill-starred Browns. Even his teammates and manager focused more on his disability than on his grit and determination, which frustrated Gray who only wished to be recognized as a ball player and not as some side-show. The resulting alienation from the team and big-league pitchers learning to exploit the weaknesses of his one-armed swing led to a disappointing .218 average and no home runs in limited playing time. With the end of WWII, baseball welcomed back its returning stars for the start of the 1946 season and forced Gray back down to the minors where he toiled for two more years before calling it quits. Though his time in the show amounted to only one short year, his true legacy came in the form of the inspiration provided to many, by visiting hospitals and rehab centers to meet with amputees and servicemen who returned with disabilities.

Here's a game from that 1945 season in which the Browns played host to the Philadelphia Athletics for a Fourth of July doubleheader. Gray started the second game while collecting three hits from the leadoff spot and helped the Browns to put up six runs on the scoreboard. Al Hollingsworth took the mound for the first 4.1 innings, giving up four runs to the Phillies on five hits and seven walks before giving way to Sam Zoldak and George Caster to sew up a 6-5 victory.

Philadelpia Athletics at **St. Louis Browns**

July 4, 1945

Batting	1	2	3	4	5	6	7	8	9	AB	R	H	RBI
Pete Gray CF										4	0	3	2
Len Schulte 2B										3	0	2	0
George McQuinn 1B										0	0	0	1
Milt Byrnes 1B										4	0	0	0
Vern Stephens SS										4	0	0	0
Gene Moore RF										4	1	1	0
Mark Christman 3B										4	1	2	2
Don Gutteridge LF										1	0	0	0
Babe Martin LF										3	1	0	0
Red Hayworth C										1	0	0	0
Frank Mancuso C										3	1	1	0
Al Hollingsworth P										1	0	0	0
Sam Zoldak P										1	0	0	0
Mike Kreevich PH										1	1	1	0
Joe Schultz PH										1	1	1	1
Runs	0	0	0	0	0	0	2	1	3				
Left on Base													

2B: Pete Gray (off Joe Berry); Gene Moore (off Joe Berry); Joe Schultz (off Joe Berry)

HR: Mark Christman (off Joe Berry)

*SF: George Mcquinn (off Joe Berry)

2-Out RBI: Schultz; Gray 2

Team LOB: 5

Reached on a FC: Babe Martin

Runners retired on the bases: Pete Gray picked off 1B by Steve Gerkin

Hint: Gerkin retired 16 batters in a row between his first and second hits allowed.

Pitching	IP	H	R	ER	BB	BF
Steve Gerkin	6	3	0	0	1	21
Joe Berry	2.2	7	6	6	0	15
Russ Christopher	0	1	0	0	0	1

SOLUTION **Pete Gray**

Batting	1	2	3	4	5	6	7	8	9	AB	R	H	RBI
Pete Gray CF	W,X		X			H		H	H,2I	4	0	3	2
Len Schulte 2B	H			X		H				3	0	2	0
George McQuinn 1B								SF,I,X		0	0	0	1
Milt Byrnes 1B	X			X		X		X		4	0	0	0
Vern Stephens SS	X			X			X	X		4	0	0	0
Gene Moore RF		X			X		H,R		X	4	1	1	0
Mark Christman 3B		X			X		H,R,2I		H,X	4	1	2	2
Don Gutteridge LF		X								1	0	0	0
Babe Martin LF					X		X		FC,R	3	1	0	0
Red Hayworth C			X							1	0	0	0
Frank Mancuso C						X	X		H,R	3	1	1	0
Al Hollingsworth P			X							1	0	0	0
Sam Zoldak P						X				1	0	0	0
Mike Kreevich PH								H,R		1	1	1	0
Joe Schultz PH									H,R,I	1	1	1	1
Runs	0	0	0	0	0	0	2	1	3				
Left on Base	1	0	0	0	0	2	0	1	1				

The Browns sent a total of 37 batters to the plate during the game, which means every position in the line-up had four plate appearances except for Pete Gray who had five. Those charged with fewer at-bats than plate appearances were McQuinn with an SF and Gray with a walk.

9th Inning

Russ Christopher faced only one hitter, the 37th and final Browns hitter of the game, Pete Gray, and allowed a hit. The hit had to produce the winning run of the game, as the 9th did not extend to three outs, so Gray picked up at least one RBI.

Schultz had only one at-bat during the game, which occurred this inning. Per his line, he had one hit, a run scored, and an RBI.

8th Inning

As Gray was the final batter in the 9th, McQuinn's lone at-bat which resulted in an SF had to occur during the 8th.

Kreevich also had his lone at-bat this inning, which resulted in a hit and run scored per his line.

Byrnes was out as he failed to reach base during the game.

7th Inning

Neither Martin nor Mancuso could have scored this inning, as no one was behind them to drive them in.

That leaves Moore and Christman to have scored this inning. Moore had to reach base on a hit.

Christman also had to reach base and drive home both himself and Moore, as again, no one behind them this inning was credited with any RBIs. Thus, Christman homered off Berry this inning.

Stephens was the 22nd batter of the game and the first to face Berry in the 7th. As he failed to reach base during the game, he was out.

Back to the 9th Inning

The two remaining runs scored belong to Martin and Mancuso. As Martin had no hits or walks during the game, he must have reached on the FC disclosed in the notes, before coming around to score.

Mancuso had to reach on his lone hit before scoring.

For Martin to have reached on the FC, someone had to be on base ahead of him. As Stephens failed to reach base during the game and Moore's lone hit was already recorded, Christman had to reach base on the second of his two hits before being forced out.

Gray's and Schultz's RBIs came with two outs, so Moore had to come to the plate this inning and was retired as his one hit was already recorded.

With Christman's two RBIs recorded in the 7th, that left Gray to have driven in two runs during the 9th.

Stephens, as mentioned above, failed to reach base during the game. Thus the 9th inning could not have extended past Martin had he come to the plate during the final frame. Stephens, therefore, accounted for the final out of the 8th.

Back to the 7th Inning

With Martin and Mancuso's only means of reaching base now recorded, both were retired during the 7th.

Back to the 8th Inning

Gray had to reach base to extend the inning. As Berry walked no one, he reached on the second of his three hits.

6th Inning

Byrnes had to be out to end the inning as he went 0-for-4.

Mancuso was charged with three at-bats during the game after entering in the 6th. He had to come to the plate this inning to account for the first of his plate appearances, and he was out as his hit was already recorded.

Zoldak was also out as he failed to reach base during his one at-bat.

That means both Gray and Schulte had to reach base to extend the inning to Byrnes. Gray reached on either a hit or the walk and Schulte reached on one of his two base hits.

5th Inning

Moore, Christman, and Martin were retired in order as none have any unrecorded hits or walks remaining.

4th Inning

Byrnes and Stephens were both out during the 4th as neither reached safely during the game.

At this time, seven consecutive outs are recorded. If the string of retired batters were to be interrupted at this point, there would not be enough batters remaining to fulfill the hint of 16 being set down in a row. So, working backward from Zoldak making the second out of the 6th, the string of 16 began with Byrnes accounting for the second out of the 1st.

With the streak of consecutive outs bookended by base hits, Schulte had to reach in the 1st on the first of his two hits and Gray got the first of his three hits in the 6th.

That leaves Gray to have drawn his walk during the 1st but was then picked off by Gerkin as disclosed in the notes to account for one of the outs during the inning.

21. From the Youngest (Joe Nuxhall)...

Joe Nuxhall became the youngest player to ever appear in a major league game when in 1944, at the age of 15, he took the mound for the Cincinnati Redlegs and threw to nine batters during an 18-0 blowout loss to the St. Louis Cardinals. During his inaugural outing, he gave up two hits, including a single to Stan Musial, and five walks while allowing five runs.

Nuxhall had caught the attention of the Reds while they scouted his father to help fill their war-depleted roster. But when the elder Nuxhall rebuffed their interest, the Reds turned their eyes to the hard-throwing 6-foot-2 high school sophomore. After obtaining clearance under child labor laws and awaiting completion of the school year, Cincinnati welcomed Nuxhall to the big-league club for his inauspicious debut on June 10, 1944.

He would wait eight years before making his next major-league appearance. During the interim, he returned to his hometown to finish high school and progressed through the Reds farm system while refining his control. By 1952, he earned his way back onto the big-league roster where he became a fixture of the rotation, starting 287 games over the next 15 seasons, all but two years with Cincinnati. His best year came in 1955 when he won 17 games and earned the first of two all-star selections.

Retiring after the 1966 season with 135 career wins, Nuxhall continued his affiliation with the Reds while providing color commentary alongside the likes of Al Michaels and Marty Brennaman for the team's radio broadcast. His 60-year association with the franchise, spanning his adolescent debut and final sign-off from the booth, cemented an endearing legacy with the city, a relationship immortalized with a bronze statue of the Ol' Lefthander at the entrance to Cincinnati's Great American Ball Park.

Here's a game from the 1955 season in which Nuxhall and the Redlegs visited the Pittsburgh Pirates for an early season contest. Eleven years removed from his debut and now in his prime at the age of 26, Nuxhall went the full nine innings for the Reds, holding the Pirates to only six hits and allowing no runs. The shutout marked the first of five that year for Nuxhall, which led the National League. He also contributed to the offense during the 5-0 victory with the first of his three home runs that year.

Cincinnati Redlegs at Pittsburgh Pirates

April 29, 1955

Batting	1	2	3	4	5	6	7	8	9	AB	R	H	RBI
Johnny Temple 2B										3	2	1	0
Ray Jablonski 3B										4	0	1	0
Ted Kluszewski 1B										4	0	2	2
Wally Post RF										4	1	1	0
Gus Bell CF										3	1	1	0
Jim Greengrass LF										4	0	1	1
Roy McMillan SS										3	0	0	1
Hobie Landrith C										4	0	1	0
Joe Nuxhall P										4	1	1	1
Runs	1	0	0	1	2	1	0	0	0				
Left on Base													

2B: Wally Post (off Max Surkont); Ted Kluszewski (off Max Surkont)

HR: Joe Nuxhall (off Max Surkont)

SF: Roy McMillan (off Vern Law)

2-Out RBI: Ted Kluszewski; Jim Greengrass

Team LOB: 4

Runners retired on the bases: Ray Jablonski thrown out at 3B for the first out of the inning; Hobie Landrith caught stealing 2B

Advanced on WP: Gus Bell

Hint: Both Johnny Temple and Gus Bell reached base on a walk before getting a base-hit.

Pitching	IP	H	R	ER	BB	BF
Max Surkont	5	7	4	4	1	22
Vern Law	3	1	1	1	1	11
Laurin Pepper	1	1	0	0	0	3

123

SOLUTION   **From the Youngest (Joe Nuxhall)...**

Batting	1	2	3	4	5	6	7	8	9	AB	R	H	RBI
Johnny Temple 2B	W,R		X		H,R		X			3	2	1	0
Ray Jablonski 3B	H,X		X		X		X			4	0	1	0
Ted Kluszewski 1B	H,I			X	H,I			X		4	0	2	2
Wally Post RF	X			H,R	X			X		4	1	1	0
Gus Bell CF	X			X		W,R		H		3	1	1	0
Jim Greengrass LF		X		H,I		X		X		4	0	1	1
Roy McMillan SS		X		X		SF,I,X			X	3	0	0	1
Hobie Landrith C		X			X	X			H,X	4	0	1	0
Joe Nuxhall P			X		H,R,I		X		X	4	1	1	1
Runs	1	0	0	1	2	1	0	0	0				
Left on Base	1	0	0	1	1	0	0	1	0				

With 36 batters having come to the plate throughout the game, each position in the line-up came to the plate four times. Those charged with fewer than four at-bats were McMillan who was credited with an SF and Temple and Bell who received the two walks allowed by the Pirates' hurlers.

9th Inning

Laurin Pepper threw to the 36th and final Redleg's batter, Joe Nuxhall, for the last out of the inning.

Pepper faced only three hitters but recorded three outs and allowed one hit. Hence, whoever reached base must have been subsequently erased.

McMillan had no hits during the game, so he did not reach base and instead accounted for the first out of the inning.

That leaves Landrith to have reached base on the one hit allowed by Pepper but was then thrown out trying to steal second as disclosed in the notes.

6th Inning

Per the notes, McMillan had an SF off Law. As the 6th is the only inning in which a run scored with Law on the mound, the SF had to occur during this frame.

The SF could not have ended the inning, so Landrith had to come to the plate this inning and was retired as his hit is already recorded.

The first batter to face Vern Law during the 6th was the 23rd hitter in the order, Bell. As he was the only hitter credited with a run scored preceding McMillan to the plate this inning, Bell had to reach base and score. At this point, we cannot be certain whether he reached on a hit or on a walk.

5th Inning

Post was the final batter to face Surkont and so was retired to end the inning.

The two runs scored this inning had to come from Temple and Nuxhall. Bell's run scored is already recorded, and Post, as noted above, was out to end the inning.

We cannot yet determine whether Temple reached on a hit or on a walk.

Nuxhall reached base only once during the game which was his home run, so that must have occurred this inning.

Kluszewski was the only hitter behind Temple credited with an RBI, so he had to drive in the second run of the inning with one of his two base hits.

Jablonski did have one hit during the game but was subsequently thrown out at third base. Whether that occurred this inning or not, Jablonski accounted for one of the outs this inning.

Landrith had to come to the plate this inning and was retired as he has no remaining hits to record.

1st Inning

The two unaccounted-for runs scored at this point belong to Temple and Post. Post could not have scored the one run during the 1st without one of the three hitters ahead of him reaching base and scoring as well. Temple, therefore, had to account for the run scored this inning, and with the hint that he walked before collecting his hit, he reached via the free pass. That means Temple reached on a hit during the 5th.

4th Inning

Post now owns the only unrecorded run scored, so he must have rounded the bases to account for the tally this inning after reaching on his lone base hit.

McMillan was out to end the inning so that Landrith could lead off the 5th.

The only hitter behind Post with an unrecorded RBI was Greengrass, so he must have driven in the run this inning with his lone hit.

Back to the 1st Inning

Like the 5th inning, Jablonski had to account for one of the three outs during the inning, even if he did reach on his lone base hit.

Kluszewski owns the final RBI to record, so he must have driven Temple home this inning on the first of his two base hits.

Post was out as his one hit is already recorded.

Back to the 6th Inning

Greengrass was out as his lone hit has now been recorded.

For Bell to be in a position to score on the SF, he must have advanced on the wild pitch disclosed in the notes and moved further along on Greengrass's out.

7th Inning

Both Nuxhall and Temple were out, as their hits and walks were already recorded.

Per the notes, Jablonski was thrown out at third base for the first out of the inning. As Nuxhall and Temple accounted for the first two outs of the inning, Jablonski was not the one to have collected the one hit off Vern Law but was simply retired to end the inning.

8th Inning

Greengrass was the 33rd and final batter to face Law, so he was out to end the inning.

Kluszewski and Post were both retired as each of their hits was already recorded.

That means Bell had to reach base to extend the inning to Greengrass for the final out. Per the hint, his walk came first, so he had to reach on a hit this inning and drew the walk during the 6th.

Back to the 4th Inning

With Bell's hit and walk now recorded, he accounted for the second out of the 4th.

Kluszewski was retired to complete his line.

Jablonski, as noted above, whether he picked up his hit or not, accounted for an out, as he was subsequently thrown out at third after reaching base. Thus, he could not have led off the 4th as the three outs are already recorded. He, therefore, ended the third with an out.

Per the notes, Jablonski was thrown out for the first out of an inning, so that had to occur in the 1st frame. During Jablonski's remaining at-bats, he accounted for either the second or third out of the inning.

With all seven hits and one walk allowed by Surkont now recorded, the remaining hitters were retired, beginning with Bell to end the 1st through Temple for the second out of the 3rd.

22.   ...To the Oldest (Satchel Paige)

Satchel Paige once asked, "How old would you be if you didn't know how old you were?" Satchel must have thought of himself as a twenty-something-year-old when in 1965 at the birth age of 58, he hurled three scoreless innings for the Kansas City Athletics, allowing only one hit, walking none, and striking out one.

The outing, which qualified Paige as the oldest player of a major league game, came 38 years after his debut with the Birmingham Black Barons of the Negro National League in 1927. His long arms and high leg kick generated a powerful fastball that bewildered hitters and dazzled the fans. During his first three years with the Barons, he fanned more batters per nine innings than any hurler in either the Negro or Major Leagues. And in 1929, he led all of baseball with 189 strikeouts in only 185.2 innings pitched compared to Lefty Grove who led the MLB with 170 Ks in 275 innings. His playful antics such as ordering his fielders to take a seat and then striking out the side, added to his legacy and turned him into a national celebrity. He leveraged that popularity in awarding his services to the highest bidders amongst the Negro, Cuban, California, Dominican Republic, Mexican, and Puerto Rican leagues, and even the House of David teams. His Satchel Paige All-Star barnstorming tours drew thousands of eager fans who clamored to witness Paige versus the white stars of the major leagues.

Not until 1948, the year after Jackie Robinson broke the color barrier, did Paige finally get the opportunity to showcase his talents in the major leagues. At the age of 41, he went 6-1 on the season with a 2.48 ERA helping Cleveland to a World Series title and becoming the first African American to appear in the Fall Classic. He spent another season with the Indians before moving on to St. Louis for three years with the Browns before taking a 12-year hiatus which culminated with that farewell appearance in 1965. Officially he won 121 games during his 21 years in the Negro and Major Leagues, but many speculate that by adding in his time with competing leagues and barnstorming tours, he must have appeared in 2,500 games and won nearly 2,000. Major League Baseball recognized that full body of work when in 1971, they inducted him into their Hall of Fame.

Here's that game from September 25, 1965, in which Satchel defied his age and entered the history books. The A's owner, Charles Finley, arranged the outing as a tribute to the Kansas City Monarchs of the Negro American League for whom Paige played seven seasons. With some of his old teammates on hand, Paige had a nearly flawless night, allowing the opposing Red Sox only one hit, a double by future Hall-of-Famer, Carl Yastrzemski. He finished after three innings with a 1-0 lead, but the A's faltered in the late innings and fell 5-2 to the visiting Red Sox.

Boston Red Sox at Kansas City Athletics

September 25, 1965

Batting	1	2	3	4	5	6	7	8	9	AB	R	H	RBI
Jim Gosger CF										4	1	1	0
Dalton Jones 3B										3	0	0	0
Frank Malzone PH-3B										1	0	0	0
Carl Yastrzemski LF										4	1	2	0
Tony Conigliaro RF										3	2	2	2
Lee Thomas 1B										3	1	1	2
Felix Mantilla 2B										4	0	1	0
Eddie Bressoud SS										4	0	0	0
Mike Ryan C										4	0	0	0
Bill Monbouquette P										4	0	0	0
Runs	0	0	0	0	0	0	2	3	0				
Left on Base													

2B: Carl Yastrzemski (off Satchel Paige)

HR: Lee Thomas (off Diego Segui); Tony Conigliaro (off John Wyatt)

2-Out RBI: Tony Conigliaro 2

Team LOB: 4

Reached on Error: Dalton Jones

Runners retired on the bases: Dalton Jones thrown out at 3B

Scored on a WP: Jim Gosger

Hint: Tony Conigliaro's first hit was sandwiched between the Red Sox committing an error and issuing a lead-off walk, but all occurred in separate innings.

Pitching	IP	H	R	ER	BB	BF
Satchel Paige	3	1	0	0	0	10
Diego Segui	4	3	2	2	1	16
Don Mossi	0.1	1	1	1	0	2
John Wyatt	0.1	2	2	2	1	4
Jack Aker	1.1	0	0	0	0	4

SOLUTION   ...To the Oldest (Satchel Paige)

Batting	1	2	3	4	5	6	7	8	9	AB	R	H	RBI
Jim Gosger CF	X		X			X		H,R		4	1	1	0
Dalton Jones 3B	E,X			X		X				3	0	0	0
Frank Malzone PH-3B								X		1	0	0	0
Carl Yastrzemski LF	H			X		X		H,R		4	1	2	0
Tony Conigliaro RF	X			H			W,R	H,R,2I		3	2	2	2
Lee Thomas 1B		X		X			H,R,2I	W		3	1	1	2
Felix Mantilla 2B		X			H		X	X		4	0	1	0
Eddie Bressoud SS		X			X		X		X	4	0	0	0
Mike Ryan C			X		X		X		X	4	0	0	0
Bill Monbouquette P			X		X			X	X	4	0	0	0
Runs	0	0	0	0	0	0	2	3	0				
Left on Base	1	0	0	1	1	0	0	1	0				

With 36 batters having come to the plate throughout the game, each position in the Red Sox's line-up came to the plate four times. Those charged with fewer than four at-bats were Conigliaro and Thomas who drew the two walks issued by the Athletics' pitchers.

1st, 2nd and 3rd Innings

Satchel Paige faced the first ten Red Sox and allowed only one hit, the double by Yastrzemski disclosed in the notes. That had to occur during the 1st as Yastrzemski had only one chance versus Paige.

The other nine hitters to face Paige during his three innings of work were all retired, the last being Gosger to end the third inning.

9th Inning

Aker recorded the final out of the inning while facing the 36th and final batter of the game for the Red Sox, Monbouquette.

The three batters preceding Monbouquette were also retired as Aker allowed no walks or hits during his appearance, Mantilla accounting for the final out of the 8th.

8th Inning

Wyatt threw to the four batters ahead of Mantilla during the 8th and gave up two hits and one walk while recording only one out. One of the hits per the notes was the home run by Conigliaro. Thomas then had to draw the walk as only he and Conigliaro drew a free pass during the game.

Of the two remaining hitters faced by Wyatt, only Yastrzemski had a hit, leaving Malzone to account for the out.

Mossi faced only two batters, allowing one hit and recording one out. The out had to come from Monbouquette as he failed to reach base during the game. That leaves Gosger who reached on the hit.

As this was Gosger's only time in which he reached base during the game, he had to score on the WP disclosed in the notes.

Yastrzemski had to score on Conigliaro's home run, allowing Conigliaro to pick up his two RBIs.

7th Inning

Ryan and Bressoud were both out at the end of the inning, as neither reached base at any point during the game.

Per the notes, Thomas homered off Segui. That had to come this inning as the 7th is the only frame in which Segui allowed any runs.

Conigliaro owns the only remaining unrecorded walk and run scored. As the only other walk, issued to Thomas, came with two outs, Conigliaro's free pass had to fulfill the hint of occurring as he led off an inning. His only other at-bat to record aside from this inning, came in the 4th when he batted third. Thus, Conigliaro had to walk this inning before coming around to score on Thomas's home run.

4th Inning

Both Jones and Yastrzemski were out to begin the inning, as neither has any unrecorded hits or walks remaining.

Conigliaro reached on a hit to complete his line.

Thomas was out to complete his batting line.

Back to the 7th

Knowing that Conigliaro led off the inning, Mantilla had to account for the first out of the 7th.

5th and 6th Innings

Mantilla led off the 5th with a base hit to complete his batting line.

The remaining batters during these two frames were retired, as the three hits and one walk allowed by Segui were already recorded.

Back to the 1st

In accordance with the hint, Jones had to reach on the error during the first inning. His only other at-bat preceding Conigliaro's first hit came in the 4th, but per the hint, the error, hit, and walk all came in separate innings.

As this was Jones' only plate appearance in which he reached base, he was subsequently thrown out at third base as disclosed in the notes.

23. 1980 Philadelphia Phillies

Prior to the arrival of two of the game's legends, the Philadelphia Phillies, despite nearly a century of play in the Major Leagues, never laid claim to a World Series title. That long stretch of futility included only two postseason appearances, the most recent coming 26 years before the club's turn of fortune.

The Phillies began planting the seeds of a revival during the 1971 off-season. They first orchestrated a trade for Steve Carlton of the St. Louis Cardinals who had just wrapped up a 20-win season and owned the single-game strikeout record of 19 at the time. But a request for an additional $5,000 on top of the Cardinal's offer for the upcoming season incensed ownership to the point of shipping Carlton off to Philadelphia in a trade. Carlton responded with the pitcher's version of the triple crown in 1972, leading the league with 27 wins, a 1.97 ERA, and 310 strikeouts while winning the first of his eventual four CY Young Awards.

They also used their second pick of the 1971 Amateur Draft to select a slugging infielder from Ohio University by the name of Mike Schmidt. Within two years, he worked his way into the Phillies starting lineup and beginning in 1974, led the National League in home runs for three consecutive seasons. Paired with the hard-hitting Greg Luzinski who averaged 25 home runs a season during his nine full campaigns in Philadelphia, the Phillies housed a powerful punch in the middle of their line-up. And with Carlton anchoring a staff that sported a 3.08 ERA, the Phillies climbed to the top of the NL Eastern Division in 1976 with 101 wins but exited postseason play after only one round.

The script repeated itself the following two seasons; winning the division title but failing to get past the NL Championship Series. Hopes of getting over the hump grew with the signing of Pete Rose during the 1978 off-season, but an injury-depleted rotation sent the Phillies stumbling to a 4th-place finish in the NL East in 1979. The two stalwarts ensured a quick recovery, however, with a convergence of award-winning performances the ensuing year, Carlton once again led the league in victories and strikeouts while posting the second-lowest ERA in capturing his third Cy Young Award. On the offensive side, Schmidt's 48 home runs, 121 RBIs, .624 slugging percentage, and 342 total bases all led the league and garnered unanimous consent for the first of his two successive MVP Awards. After rolling to 91 regular season wins and the Division title, the Phillies knocked out the Houston Astros in five games to advance to the World Series where they defeated the Kansas City Royals to claim the franchise's first Championship since their inception in 1883.

Here's a game from that Championship season, pitting the Phillies against NL East rivals, the Chicago Cubs. Though Schmidt highlighted the offensive attack with two home runs, four others contributed two hits apiece, including veterans Rose, Luzinski, and Larry Bowa, as well as rookie, Lonnie Smith. The seven runs proved more than enough with Carlton shutting out the Cubs over his seven innings of work, allowing only four hits and striking out 11 while walking no one. Dickie Noles upheld the shutout in his two innings to close out the 7-0 victory.

Philadephia Phillies at Chicago Cubs

    May 31, 1980

Batting	1	2	3	4	5	6	7	8	9	AB	R	H	RBI
Lonnie Smith RF										4	2	2	1
Pete Rose 1B										4	1	2	1
Del Unser 1B										1	0	1	0
Mike Schmidt 3B										3	2	2	3
John Vukovich 3B										1	0	0	0
Greg Luzinski LF										5	0	2	1
Bob Boone C										4	0	0	0
Gary Maddox CF										5	0	0	0
Larry Bowa SS										4	1	2	0
Manny Trillo 2B										3	1	0	0
Steve Carlton P										2	0	0	0
Greg Gross PH										0	0	0	0
Runs	0	0	3	3	0	0	1	0	0				
Left on Base													

2B: Larry Bowa (off Willie Hernandez); Lonnie Smith (off Willie Hernandez)

HR: Mike Schmidt 2 (off Bill Caudill and off Willie Hernandez)

SH: Steve Carlton (off Willie Hernandez)

2-Out RBI: Greg Luzinski

Team LOB: 8

Reached on a FC: Bob Boone

Runners retired on the bases: Lonnie Smith thrown out stealing 2B

Hint: Manny Trillo scored on an outfield error.

Pitching	IP	H	R	ER	BB	BF
Willie Hernandez	3.1	7	5	5	2	18
Lynn McGlothen	2.2	2	1	1	1	11
Bill Caudill	2.0	1	1	1	1	8
Doug Capilla	1.0	1	0	0	1	5

SOLUTION   1980 Philadelphia Phillies

Batting	1	2	3	4	5	6	7	8	9	AB	R	H	RBI
Lonnie Smith RF	W,X		H,R	H,R,I		X		X		4	2	2	1
Pete Rose 1B	H		H,R,I	X		X				4	1	2	1
Del Unser 1B									H	1	0	1	0
Mike Schmidt 3B	X		H,R,2I	W			H,R,I			3	2	2	3
John Vukovich 3B									X	1	0	0	0
Greg Luzinski LF	X		H,X	H,I			X		X	5	0	2	1
Bob Boone C		X	FC	X			X		W	4	0	0	0
Gary Maddox CF		X	X		X		X		X	5	0	0	0
Larry Bowa SS		H		H,R	X			X		4	1	2	0
Manny Trillo 2B		X		W,R	X			X		3	1	0	0
Steve Carlton P			X	SH,X		X				2	0	0	0
Greg Gross PH									W	0	0	0	0
Runs	0	0	3	3	0	0	1	0	0				
Left on Base	1	1	1	2	0	0	0	1	2				

With 42 batters having come to the plate throughout the game, the top six hitters in the Phillies' line-up each came to the plate five times while the bottom three stepped into the box only four times. Those charged with fewer at-bats than plate appearances were Carlton with a sacrifice hit and Smith, Boone, Trillo, and the third and ninth positions with walks.

9th Inning

Gary Maddox was the 42nd and final batter of the game for the Phillies, so he was retired to end the inning.

Of the five batters Capilla faced, one reached on a hit and another on a walk. The former had to come from Unser as this was his only plate appearance and opportunity to collect his base hit. The latter had to come from Boone as he was the only hitter amongst the five faced by Capilla to have walked during the game.

That leaves Vukovich to have accounted for the first out of the inning during his lone at-bat of the game and Luzinski for the second out.

7th and 8th Innings

Mike Schmidt was the 30th batter of the game for the Phillies and the first to face Caudill to open the 7th. Per the notes, that lone at-bat he had versus Caudill resulted in a home run.

The only other batter to reach base against Caudill came from a walk. Neither Luzinski nor Maddox drew a walk during the game, so they were both out during the 7th. Boone's walk is already accounted for, so he was out as well.

Of the four batters who came to the plate during the 8th, three have unrecorded walks: Trillo, Gross, and Smith. As the 8th inning was Gross's only plate appearance, he had to earn the free pass here, leaving the other three to account for the outs.

3rd and 4th Innings

Smith has two unrecorded runs scored. Though not yet able to determine how he reached base, he had to account for a run scored in each of the two innings.

Smith, as the 19th batter to come to the plate during the game, was the first batter to face McGlothen during the 4th. Schmidt's home run off Hernandez, therefore, had to occur during the 3rd, as his plate appearance in the 4th came against McGlothen.

With Smith reaching base and eventually scoring, he had to account for the one run that was charged to McGlothen. The other two runs scored during the 4th were charged to Hernandez, meaning those two runs had to score ahead of Smith. That leaves Bowa and Trillo as the only possible candidates for the other two runs scored during the 4th. Bowa had to reach on one of his two hits and Trillo on his walk.

Rose now owns the only unrecorded run scored, so he had to reach on one of his two base hits during the 3rd and come around to score on Schmidt's home run.

Schmidt picked up one of his three RBIs during the 7th, so he could only have driven in two runs with the homer here in the 3rd. That means Rose had to pick up the other RBI as Smith did not drive himself in. Rose had no extra-base hits though, so for Smith to be in scoring position, he must have reached base during the 3rd on his double off Hernandez.

Per the hint, Trillo scored on an outfield error, so no one was credited with an RBI. The two remaining RBIs to be credited belong to Smith and Luzinski. Smith had to collect his second hit of the game during the 4th to drive in the run. Luzinski collected one of his two hits as well during the 4th to drive in Smith.

Carlton may have moved Bowa and Trillo forward with his sacrifice during the 4th but regardless, he accounted for one of the outs during the 4th.

Boone was retired following Luzinski, as his walk was already recorded. Luzinski's RBI came with two outs, so Boone had to end the inning.

That means either Rose or Schmidt had to reach base to extend the inning to Boone. Rose has an unrecorded hit, but the two hits allowed by McGlothen were already recorded. Thus, Rose was out, and it was Schmidt who reached base on the walk issued by McGlothen.

5th and 6th Innings

The remaining six batters to face McGlothen beginning with Maddox in the 5th and ending with Rose in the 6th, were all retired, as the two hits and one walk allowed by the hurler were accounted for.

1st Inning

Smith reached on a walk to complete his line. This had to be the inning in which he was caught stealing though, as he came around to score the other two times he reached base.

Rose had to reach on the first of his two hits to complete his line.

Schmidt was out to complete his line.

<u>Back to the 3rd Inning</u>

Boone reached base at some point in the game on an FC. That could not have occurred during the 4th as he ended the inning, nor could it have come in the 7th as no one was on base ahead of him. He walked during the 9th. With two outs already recorded in the 1st, he wouldn't be able to reach on the FC during that frame either, so the only remaining possibility was the 3rd.

As Schmidt cleared the bases with a home run, Luzinski had to reach on the first of his two hits to put Boone's FC in order.

Maddox was then out to end the inning so that Bowa could lead off the 4th.

Carlton led off the inning with the first out, as he failed to reach base during the game. As the 4th was the only inning in which Carlton had runners on base during his at-bat, the SH had to occur during that frame.

Of the remaining at-bats, Luzinski was retired in the 1st to end the inning and complete his line. Bowa reached on the first of his two hits during the 2nd to complete his line, leaving Boone, Maddox, and Trillo to account for the three outs.

24. 2011 Texas Rangers

The Texas Rangers, who began as the expansion Washington Senators in 1961, failed to make a World Series appearance during their first forty-nine years in the American League. During that span of futility, they won only one postseason game despite capturing three AL West Division crowns between 1996 and 1999. Not until 2010 after taking a flyer on a player beset by injuries and substance abuse problems did the Rangers finally earn another chance to get over the hump.

Though selected first overall in the 1999 amateur draft, Josh Hamilton waited seven years before making his major league debut, sitting out three years on baseball's restricted list as he wrestled with personal issues. After a lackluster rookie season in Cincinnati in 2007, the Reds packaged him in a trade with Texas, where the once-can't-miss prospect, at last, lived up to those tall expectations from the past. In his first season with the Rangers, he led the league in RBIs (130) and total bases (331) while earning his first All-Star appearance. Following an injury-riddled 2009, his slash line of .359/.411/.633 combined with 32 home runs and 100 RBIs in 2010 garnered the MVP Award. Mixed in with a potent lineup, including Nelson Cruz, Vladimir Guerrero, Ian Kinsler, and Michael Young, the Rangers recorded 90 regular season wins to secure their first AL pennant and a trip to the Fall Classic.

After falling to the San Francisco Giants in five games during the championship match-up, the front office immediately set upon improving the Rangers chances for the following season. Though Guerrero auctioned off his 29 home runs and 115 RBIs to another team, the Rangers countered with their free-agent signing of Adrian Beltre and a trade for Mike Napoli. Touting a batting order with five hitters collecting 25 or more home runs; Kinsler (32), Beltre (32), Hamilton (25), Cruz (29), and Napoli (30), along with Young who led the league with 213 hits, the Rangers bettered their 2010-win total by six. A healthy rotation which saw each of the five starters, C.J. Wilson, Colby Leis, Derek Holland, Matt Harrison, and Alexi Ogando, take the mound for at least 29 games and contribute a minimum of 13 wins helped in securing a second pennant and another chance at the championship.

Though defeating the St. Louis Cardinals in three of the first five games of the Series, and twice being only one strike away from winning game six, the Rangers once again fell short and remain one of only six current franchises to have never hoisted the World Series trophy.

Here's the Ranger's opening day game from that 2011 season in which they hosted the Boston Red Sox. The offense provided a forewarning of their potency with ten hits, including three home runs and pushing nine runners across the plate. C.J. Wilson toed the rubber for the first 5.2 innings and allowed only two earned runs on six hits and two walks while striking out six. Four other hurlers followed Wilson to the mound, giving up only one additional run to secure the 9–5 victory and the first of six consecutive wins to begin the season.

138

Boston Red Sox at **Texas Rangers**

April 1, 2011

Batting	1	2	3	4	5	6	7	8	9	AB	R	H	RBI
Ian Kinsler 2B										5	1	1	1
Elvis Andrus SS										4	1	1	1
Josh Hamilton LF-CF										4	0	1	1
Adrian Beltre 3B										4	1	1	0
Michael Young DH										5	0	0	0
Nelson Cruz RF										3	2	2	1
Mike Napoli 1B										3	2	2	3
Yorvit Torrealba C										4	1	1	0
Julio Borbon CF										1	0	0	0
David Murphy PH-LF										1	1	1	2
Runs	1	1	0	3	0	0	0	4	x				
Left on Base													

2B: David Murphy (off Daniel Bard); Elvis Andrus (off Daniel Bard); Josh Hamilton (off Daniel Bard)

HR: Ian Kinsler (off Jon Lester); Nelson Cruz (off Jon Lester); Mike Napoli (off Jon Lester)

HBP: Julio Borbon (by Jon Lester); Elvis Andrus (by Jon Lester)

HIDP: Josh Hamilton

2-Out RBI: Mike Napoli 3; Elvis Andrus; Josh Hamilton

Team LOB: 8

Reached on Error: Elvis Andrus

Hint: Jon Lester suffered throug a stretch of wildness, hitting two batters in one inning and then issuing his lone walk the following inning.

Pitching	IP	H	R	ER	BB	BF
Jon Lester	5.1	6	5	5	1	25
Matt Albers	1	0	0	0	1	4
Dennys Reyes	0	0	0	0	1	1
Dan Wheeler	0.2	0	0	0	0	2
Daniel Bard	0.2	4	4	4	1	7
Tim Wakefield	0.1	0	0	0	1	2

SOLUTION   **2011 Texas Rangers**

Batting	1	2	3	4	5	6	7	8	9	AB	R	H	RBI
Ian Kinsler 2B	H,R,I		X		X	X		X		5	1	1	1
Elvis Andrus SS	E		X		HBP		X	H,R,I		4	1	1	1
Josh Hamilton LF-CF	XX			X	X		W	H,I		4	0	1	1
Adrian Beltre 3B	X			H,R	X		X	W		4	1	1	0
Michael Young DH		X		X		X	X	X		5	0	0	0
Nelson Cruz RF		H,R,I		H,R		W		X		3	2	2	1
Mike Napoli 1B		X		H,R,3I		H		W,R		3	2	2	3
Yorvit Torrealba C		X		X		X		H,R		4	1	1	0
Julio Borbon CF			X		HBP	W				1	0	0	0
David Murphy PH-LF								H,R,2I		1	1	1	2
Runs	1	1	0	3	0	0	0	4	x				
Left on Base	0	0	0	0	2	3	1	2	x				

With 41 batters having come to the plate throughout the game, the Rangers went through their full line-up four times. The top five in the order came to the plate an additional time. Those charged with fewer at-bats than plate appearances included Julio Borbon and Elvis Andrus who were hit by a pitch. Josh Hamilton, Adrian Beltre, Nelson Cruz, Mike Napoli, and someone in the ninth spot drew the walks.

8th Inning

Michael Young was the 41st and final batter of the evening for the Rangers, so he was retired to end the inning.

Of the two batters Wakefield faced, he retired one and walked the other. With Young already accounting for the out, Beltre drew the walk.

Bard preceded Wakefield on the mound and threw to seven hitters, all in the 8th inning. Per the notes, he allowed a barrage of doubles, one each to Murphy, Andrus, and Hamilton.

As this was Murphy's only plate appearance during the game, his double had to drive in the two runs he was credited for, and he eventually had to come around to score.

Kinsler's lone hit was his home run off Lester, so he was out during the 8th.

Of the remaining three batters Bard faced, starting with Cruz, one had to account for the first out of the inning and the other two had to come home on Murphy's double. With Murphy also scoring, that accounts for three of the four runs tallied this inning. As Andrus reached base ahead of Hamilton and Beltre, he had to account for the fourth run scored during the inning.

With Murphy having driven in the two runners on ahead of him, the other two RBIs had to come from Andrus and Hamilton as no one else behind Murphy, other than Kinsler, was credited with an RBI. But Kinsler's had to come via his HR off Lester.

6th and 7th Innings

Wheeler faced the 32nd and 33rd hitters in the line-up during the 7th, Beltre and Young, and retired them both as he allowed no hits or walks during his brief appearance.

Reyes pitched to only one batter, Hamilton, and walked him.

Albers came into the game during the 6th with one out and faced only four hitters beginning with the 26th in the line-up, Torrealba. He gave up only one walk, which had to be issued to Borbon as he was the only one amongst the four to have drawn a free pass.

That leaves Torrealba and Kinsler to account for the final two outs of the 6th, and Andrus who was retired leading off the 7th. If Andrus had reached on the error while Albers was on the mound, Albers would have been credited with only 0.2 innings pitched, so Andrus had to reach on the error at some other point.

4th Inning

Napoli collected three RBIs during the game. At least one had to come during the 3rd as he could only collect two at most during the 1st and 2nd innings. The four in the 8th were already accounted for.

The only other two remaining RBIs belong to Kinsler and Cruz, both coming off solo home runs. Note that all three of Napoli's RBIs came with two outs. With Cruz having no 2-out RBIs and batting directly ahead of Napoli, he could not have driven in any runs during the same frame as Napoli.

There is also no plausible scenario in which Kinsler connected for his home run this inning. If Kinsler had led off the 4th with the solo shot, the inning could not have extended past Young. Andrus may have reached on the error, but as his run scored is already accounted for, he would have had to be retired on the bases for the first out so as not to score again. Hamilton and Young had no remaining means of reaching base and would then have accounted for the other two outs. If Napoli's home run had accounted for the first run of the inning, both Young and Cruz would have had to be retired to allow for Napoli's 2-out RBI, but neither Torrealba nor Borbon could have reached base following Napoli, as Kinsler's home run came with the bases empty. Thus, Napoli now had to account for all three RBIs this inning.

Kinsler's run scored would come on his home run and Andrus' tally was already recorded, leaving Beltre and Cruz to have scored on Napoli's home run. Beltre's walk was already recorded, so he reached on a hit. We will have to come back to Cruz to determine how he reached.

Napoli's RBIs came with two outs. Hamilton's walk and hit were already recorded, so he accounted for the first out. Young failed to reach base during the game, so he was the second.

1st and 2nd Innings

Cruz's home run could not have come in the first. With only one run scored in the inning, no one else could have scored or been on base ahead of Cruz. Thus, Kinsler's solo home run came in the 1st and Cruz's during the 2nd.

Back to the 8th Inning

As mentioned above, of the three remaining batters to have faced Bard during the inning, two reached base and scored while the other accounted for the first out of the inning. With Cruz's two runs scored now recorded, he did not tally a run during the 8th and was therefore retired.

That leaves Napoli and Torrealba to have scored the first two runs of the inning. Napoli, being the only one of the two to have drawn a walk during the game, reached on the free pass issued by Bard and Torrealba reached on his lone hit.

5th and 6th Innings

With Torrealba's hit now recorded, he must have been retired to end the 4th inning. That leaves Borbon to lead off the 5th. We cannot yet determine the outcome of Borbon's at-bat, but Kinsler had to follow him with an out as his hit was already recorded.

Hamilton, Beltre, and Young were all retired during either the 5th or 6th as none have any unrecorded hits or walks remaining. With two outs already recorded in the 6th, however, only the last of these three could have come to the plate that inning. That leaves Hamilton and Beltre to account for the second and third outs of the 5th and Young getting charged for the first out of the 6th.

Bourbon had to reach base during the 5th to extend the frame to Beltre. As his walk was already recorded, he was hit by a pitch from Lester.

Relying on the hint, Andrus then reached after being hit by a pitch as well.

Both Cruz and Napoli had to reach base during the 6th to extend the inning to Kinsler for the final out. Relying on the hint once again, that Lester issued his lone walk after having hit two batters and noting that Napoli's walk was already recorded, Cruz drew the base on balls while Napoli reached on the second of his two hits.

Briefly going back to the 4th inning, with Cruz's walk recorded in the 6th, he had to reach base on a hit during the 4th.

3rd Inning

If Andrus had reached base to lead off the 4th, he would have scored ahead of Beltre, but his run scored was already recorded. If he had led off with an out, the inning could not have extended past Young. He was therefore out to end the 3rd, allowing Hamilton to lead off the 4th.

Both Kinsler and Borbon were out to complete their batting lines.

2nd Inning

Young, Napoli, and Torrealba were all retired to complete their lines and account for the three outs during the inning.

1st Inning

Andrus had to reach base on the error disclosed in the notes, as this is his last plate appearance to record.

Beltre ended the inning with an out to complete his line.

That leaves Hamilton to have hit into the DP this inning.

25.   1997 Florida Marlins

In 1997, the Florida Marlins in only their fifth year of existence, made history in becoming, at the time, the quickest expansion club to win a World Series crown and the first to claim the title as a wild-card berth. In their sixth season, they once again set a historic mark by falling back into the cellar with 108 losses as reigning Champions. The roller coaster of seasons began in 1993 when the owner of the NFL Miami Dolphins, Wayne Huizenga, successfully campaigned for an MLB expansion franchise to fill his Pro Player Stadium during the summer months. After suffering four losing seasons to begin their stay in the NL East, Huizenga grew impatient and doubled his payroll while securing free agents, Kevin Brown, Al Leiter, Alex Fernandez, Bobby Bonilla, and Moises Alou. He also kept Gary Sheffield in the fold with an extension that made the All-Star outfielder one of the league's highest-paid players. To manage his cast of mercenaries, Huizenga coaxed Jim Leyland away from Pittsburgh with yet another lucrative contract.

The hired guns certainly contributed to the Marlins' quick turnaround, especially from the mound. Fernandez led the rotation with 17 wins, and Brown chipped in another 16 along with his ERA of 2.69. An additional spark came from freshman hurler, Livan Hernandez who won his first nine decisions to tie Whitey Ford's record and finish second on the Rookie of the Year ballot. On the offensive side, though Bonilla and Sheffield both saw drops from their prior-year production, they joined Alou in generating an OPS in excess of .845. The balanced attack produced the second-best run differential in the National League and propelled the Marlins to their first winning season with 92 victories and a wild-card berth to the postseason.

After sweeping the San Francisco Giants in the first round, they knocked off the heavily-favored Atlanta Braves in six games with the rookie Hernandez winning two of the contests and taking home the NLCS MVP Award. Hernandez repeated his performance in the World Series with two more wins and MVP honors, as the Marlins defeated the Cleveland Indians in a thrilling seventh game that ended with Edgar Renteria driving home Craig Counsel for the winning run in the bottom of the 11th inning.

But long before uncorking the champagne bottles in celebration of the championship, Huizenga had grown frustrated in his attempts to secure public financing for the construction of a new baseball-only facility. Faced with the financial repercussions of his spending spree and little hopes of a new park, he quickly began dismantling the team, beginning with a trade of Alou, less than one month after the final out of the WS. The fire-sale continued until the payroll was stripped to a grand total of $16 million, with Renteria and Hernandez as the only remaining starters from the prior campaign on the roster at the end of the 1998 season.

Here's a late-season game from that 1997 campaign in which the Marlins hosted the Colorado Rockies. In a battle of offensive firepower, the Marlins came out on top, 9–6, with home runs from Sheffield, Alou, Bonilla, and Jeff Conine. Kirt Ojala started for the home team but got the hook after only three innings as the Rockies countered with their own barrage of fireworks. They touched Ojala for four runs on six hits and two walks before he gave way to Antonio Alfonseca who gave up another two runs in his two innings for work. Felix Heredia and Jay Powell split the final four frames and completely shut down the Rockies, allowing no hits or runs to secure the victory.

Colorado Rockies at **Florida Marlins**

September 16, 1997

Batting	1	2	3	4	5	6	7	8	9	AB	R	H	RBI
Devon White CF										2	1	1	0
Jim Eisenreich PH										1	0	0	0
John Wehner PH										0	0	0	0
Kurt Abbott PH										0	0	0	0
Edgar Renteria SS										4	1	1	0
Gary Sheffield RF										4	2	2	1
Bobby Bonilla 3B										5	2	3	5
Jeff Conine 1B										3	1	1	1
Cliff Floyd PH-1B										1	0	0	0
Moises Alou LF										4	1	1	1
Charles Johnson C										4	0	0	0
Craig Counsel 2B										4	0	1	0
John Cangelosi PH-CF										3	1	3	0
Runs	1	0	0	3	0	1	0	0	4				
Left on Base													

2B: Bobby Bonilla (off Frank Castillo)

HR: Gary Sheffield (off Frank Castillo); Moises Alou (off Frank Castillo); Jeff Conine (off Frank Castillo);
Bobby Bonilla (off Jerry Dipoto)

SH: Edgar Renteria (off Frank Castillo); John Wehner (off Darren Holmes); Kurt Abbott (off Jerry Dipoto)

HIDP: Edgar Renteria

2-Out RBI: Bobby Bonilla 5

Team LOB: 5

Reached on a FC: Edgar Renteria

Runners retired on the bases: Craig Counsell thrown out at home on a FC

Bobby Bonilla scored on a WP to Moises Alou

Hint: *Renteria's SH immediately followed a hit, while his hit immediately followed a SH.*

Pitching	IP	H	R	ER	BB	BF
Frank Castillo	6	9	5	5	0	26
Darren Holmes	1	2	0	0	0	5
Mike DeJean	1	0	0	0	0	3
Jerry Dipoto	0.2	2	4	4	2	6

SOLUTION   1997 Florida Marlins

Batting	1	2	3	4	5	6	7	8	9	AB	R	H	RBI
Devon White CF	H,R		X							2	1	1	0
Jim Eisenreich PH					X					1	0	0	0
John Wehner PH							SH,X			0	0	0	0
Kurt Abbott PH									SH,X	0	0	0	0
Edgar Renteria SS	SH,X		XX		X		H		FC,R	4	1	1	0
Gary Sheffield RF	X			H,R,I	H		X		W,R	4	2	2	1
Bobby Bonilla 3B	H,I			H,R	X		X		H,R,4I	5	2	3	5
Jeff Conine 1B	X			X		H,R,I				3	1	1	1
Cliff Floyd PH-1B								X		1	0	0	0
Moises Alou LF		X		H,R,I		X		X		4	1	1	1
Charles Johnson C		X		X		X		X		4	0	0	0
Craig Counsel 2B		X		X		X			H,X	4	0	1	0
John Cangelosi PH-CF			H		H		H		W,R	3	1	3	0
Runs	1	0	0	3	0	1	0	0	4				
Left on Base	1	0	0	0	2	0	2	0	0				

With 40 batters having come to the plate throughout the game, the Marlins went through their full line-up four times. The top four positions in the order came to the plate an additional time. Those charged with fewer at-bats than plate appearances include Wehner, Abbott, and Renteria who all had sacrificed hits during the game, and Sheffield and Cangelosi who drew walks.

9th Inning

Underline: 9th Inning

9<u>th</u> Inning

9th Inning

Bobby Bonilla was the 40th and final batter of the game for the Marlins. Per the notes, he homered off Dipoto who faced the six batters who came to the plate during the inning. Of those six batters, only Bonilla and Sheffield were credited with RBIs. Sheffield's lone RBI, however, will come with his home run off Castillo, so Bonilla drove in all four runs this inning.

Of the six batters Dipoto faced, four of them scored. While Bonilla scored one of those, Cangelosi, Renteria, and Sheffield had to account for the others, as neither Abbott nor Counsel was credited with any runs scored. Cangelosi and Sheffield had to reach on their walks to account for the two free passes issued by Dipoto. Renteria reached by either the FC or a hit, but we will come back once we can determine with certainty.

Abbott's SH had to occur this inning as this was his only opportunity to face Dipoto.

146

8th Inning

DeJean faced only three batters in his one inning of work and gave up no hits or walks, so Floyd, Alou, and Johnson were all retired.

7th Inning

Cangelosi was the 27th hitter of the game for the Marlins and the first to face Holmes in the 7th. As Cangelosi reached base during each of his at-bats and the walk was already recorded, he collected one of his hits this inning.

Wehner's only plate appearance resulted in an SH off Holmes, so he moved Cangelosi over but accounted for the first out of the inning.

Bonilla, the fifth and final batter to face Holmes, accounted for the final out of the inning for Conine to lead off the 8th.

6th Inning

Counsel was the 26th and final batter to face Castillo to end the 6th inning.

Johnson failed to reach base during the game, so he accounted for the second out of the inning.

The Marlins scored one run this inning, so either Conine or Alou had to reach base this inning so that at the very least, the inning could be extended. Between the two of them, however, they each reached base only once during the game on a home run. Thus, one of the two had to homer this inning off Castillo. The other had to account for the first out of the inning to save their homer for another inning.

That leaves Bonilla to have made the final out of the 5th inning.

4th Inning

With Bonilla accounting for the final out of the 5th, Renteria and Sheffield had to come to the plate during that inning as well. If both were retired, White would have had to end the 4th with an out for Renteria to lead off the 5th. If either Renteria or Sheffield reached base during the 5th, Eisenreich, who pinch hit for White, would have stepped into the batter's box that inning. Under either scenario, White did not account for one of the three runs scored in the 4th. That leaves Sheffield and Bonilla to have both scored this inning with the third run coming from either Conine or Alou, depending on who hit the home run during the 6th.

White then had to tally his run scored during the 1st inning. Sheffield collected only one RBI during the game which came on his home run. With White on base ahead of him in the 1st, the homer could not have occurred during the opening frame, but rather here in the 4th.

Bonilla had to reach base on one of his three hits. As mentioned before, the third run of the inning came on a home run from either Conine or Alou. Both were solo shots, however, as each collected only one RBI during the game. Thus, Bonilla had to score prior to the home run. Per the notes, he did score on a wild pitch, so that must have occurred this inning. That the wild pitch occurred while Alou was at the plate, means Bonilla was still on base after Conine's at-bat. Thus, Conine was retired this inning, and Alou hit the home run.

Johnson was out as he went hitless for the game.

Back to the 6th Inning

With Alou having homered during the 4th, he was retired in the 6th and Conine hit his solo shot off Castillo.

1st Inning

As noted above, White accounted for the run scored this inning, so he had to reach base on his hit.

The only unrecorded RBI at this point belongs to Bonilla so he had to drive in White this inning with the first of his three hits. As all of Bonilla's five RBIs came with two outs, both Renteria and Sheffield were retired ahead of him.

Conine was out to complete his batting line.

2nd and 3rd Innings

Renteria could not have reached base ahead of Sheffield's home run during the 4th inning or he would have scored. Nor could he have led off the inning with an out or Alou would have been credited with a 2-out RBI on his home run. Thus, Renteria was the final out of the 3rd.

White was out as well, as his hit was already recorded.

Cangelosi as noted before, reached base during each at-bat, so he collected another one of his hits this inning.

We now have only three spots in the order: Alou, Johnson, and Counsel to account for the three outs in the 2nd and another out in the 3rd. The only plausible scenario is that Renteria hit into the double play to end the 3rd and the three aforementioned hitters were retired in order during the 2nd.

Back to the 4th and 9th Innings

At some point, Counsel reached on a base hit but was then thrown out at home on an FC. That could not have unfolded during either the 2nd or 6th as no one batted behind Counsel during those frames. Nor could it have occurred during the 4th. If Counsel reached base during the 4th, Cangelosi would have followed with a hit, but White's batting line was finished after his at-bat in the 3rd, and did not come to the plate during the 4th.

That leaves the 9th inning as the only other opportunity for Counsel's base hit and being thrown out at home.

Counsel was then retired to end the 4th and complete his line.

As both hits allowed by Dipoto are now recorded, Renteria had to reach on the FC during the 9th.

5th Inning

Cangelosi reached on the second of his three hits to complete his batting line.

Eisenreich was out, as he was retired in his only at-bat.

Using the hint regarding the timing of Renteria's SH and hit and seeing how the game has thus unfolded, his SH had to come during the 1st, his hit during the 7th, leaving him to be retired here in the 5th.

Sheffield had to reach base on the second of his two hits during the 5th to extend the inning to Bonilla. Sheffield was then out during the 7th to complete his batting line.

A Note to the Reader

I designed these puzzles with the hopes of providing you, the reader, with an entertaining means to develop an appreciation of the box score and discover how to unlock its hidden secrets. Now that you have finished the book, I would love to hear your thoughts as to whether these pages have accomplished that goal. Did you enjoy the puzzles? Were they too difficult or not challenging enough? Were the solutions provided to each puzzle easy to follow? Most importantly, is there anything I could do to improve the experience?

I would greatly appreciate it If you could leave an honest review on Amazon. Your candid thoughts will not only assist me in designing future puzzles but also help other customers in making an informed purchasing decision.

Acknowledgments and References

I owe a great debt of gratitude to Sports Reference LLC who maintain an incredible archive of data at baseball-reference.com. Any information in this book related to individual games, including the box scores, players' season and/or career statistics, and team records is attributable to this extraordinary website. If you are so inclined to challenge or dispute any of the solutions provided to the puzzles, I invite you to visit their site and review their play by play. The site also provided helpful links to player biographies at Society for Baseball Research (SABR).

Introduction
The Man in the Crowd: Confessions of a Sports Addict, by Stanley Cohen
Baseball in the Garden of Eden, by John Thorn
The First Baseball Box Score Ever Recorded, by H.H. Westlake at *Baseball Magazine*

Murderer's Row - 1927 New York Yankees
Statmuse: *The St. Louis Maroons Have the Highest Run Differential by a Team in a Season.*
Murderer's Row and Beyond, by Pat Doyle at *Baseball Almanac*
Murderer's Row: Baseball Terminology, by Travis Coverston at *The Baseball Journal*

The Big Red Machine – 1975 and 1976 Cincinnati Reds
The Great Eight, MLB.com/Reds/Hall-of-Fame
Big Red Machine, Wikipedia

Jackie Robinson and the Brooklyn Dodgers
Jackie Robinson, written by Rick Swaine at Society for American Baseball Research (SABR)
Pee Wee Reese, written by Rob Edelman at SABR
Gil Hodges, written by John Saccoman at SABR
Don Newcombe, written by Russell Bergtold at SABR
Roy Campanella, written by Rick Swaine at SABR
Duke Snider, written by Warren Jacobs at SABR

2001 Seattle Mariners
A Midsummer Dream, by Josh Hill at Fansided.com
2001 Seattle Mariners Were One of Sport's Biggest Letdowns, by Stuart Mahoney at Bleacherreport.com
Moneyball - 2002 Oakland A's
Moneyball: The Art of Winning an Unfair Game, by Michael Lewis

Hank Greenberg
Hank Greenberg: The Story of My Life, by Hank Greenberg with Ira Berkow
Hank Greenberg, written by Scott Ferkovich at SABR

Harmon Killebrew
Harmon Killebrew, written by Joseph Wancho at SABR
List of Major League Baseball Progressive Career home runs, Wikipedia

The Miracle Mets - 1969 New York Mets
Can't Anybody Here Play This Game? by Jimmy Breslin

Shoeless Joe Jackson
Fall From Grace: The Truth and Tragedy of Shoeless Joe Jackson, by Tim Hornbaker

Miguel Cabrera
Venezuelan Bust, Baseball Boom, by Milton H Jamail
MLB Players by Birthplace During the 2022 Season, Baseball Almanac
Miguel Cabrera, Baseball Reference
Miguel Cabrera Biography, TheFamousPeople.com

2018 Boston Red Sox
2018 Boston Red Sox Season, Wikipedia
The 2018 Red Sox are World Series Champions – and Officially One of the Best Teams of All Time, by Zach Kram at The Ringer.com
Dave Dombrowski, Wikipedia
2016 Chicago Cubs
World Series 2016: Here's how the NL Champion Chicago Cubs Were Built, by Mike Axisa at cbssports.com
The 2012 Chicago Cub's On-Field Payroll is the Lowest in Seven Years, by Brett Taylor at Bleachernation.com

1995 Atlanta Braves
Who Has the Most Consecutive Postseason Appearances, at MLB.com

Casey Stengel
National Baseball Hall of Fame
Casey Stengel, written by Bill Bishop at SABR

Frank Robinson
Frank Robinson, written by Maxwell Kates at SABR
List of Major League Baseball Progressive Career home runs, Wikipedia

2017 Houston Astros
2017 Houston Astros Season, Wikipedia
The Houston Astros' Cheating Scandal: What Happened, by Neil Vigdor of the New York Times

Joe Charboneau
Joe Charboneau, written by Paul Hofmann at SABR
Super Joe: A Legend in His Own Time, by Steve Wulf

1993 Toronto Blue Jays
This Day in History, October 23, 1993, at History.com

Pete Gray

Pete Gray, written by Mel Marmer at SABR

Pete Gray Overcame a Childhood Accident to Make History, by John Powers at Baseball.org

Joe Nuxhall

Joe Nuxhall, written by Ryan Borgemenke at SABR

How a 15-year-old Pitched for the Reds, by Thomas Harrigan at MLB.com

Satchel Paige

Satchel Paige, written by Larry Tye at SABR

September 25, 1965: Satchel Paige Pitches Three Scoreless Inning at Age 59, written by Mike Huber at SABR

Satchel Paige – Wikipedia

1980 Philadelphia Phillies

Mike Schmidt, written by Steve Ferenchick and Henry Kirn at SABR

Steve Carlton, written by Cosme Vivanco at SABR

2011 Texas Rangers

Josh Hamilton, Baseball Reference

1997 Florida Marlins

1997: A Blockbuster of a Binge, The Online Book of Baseball

1997 World Series, Wikipedia

Made in the USA
Monee, IL
22 November 2023